THE LOONLINESS OF A DEEP SEA DIVER

THE
LOONLINESS
OF A DEEP SEA
DIVER

David Harrison Beckett,
My Autobiography

David Harrison Beckett
and Paul Zanon

First published by Pitch Publishing, 2016

Pitch Publishing
A2 Yeoman Gate
Yeoman Way
Durrington
BN13 3QZ
www.pitchpublishing.co.uk

A CIP catalogue record is available for this book
from the British Library.

ISBN 978-1-78531-120-8

Typesetting and origination by Pitch Publishing

Printed by TJ International Ltd, Padstow, Cornwall, UK

Contents

Dedication

To my long-suffering wife of
43 years – Jenny.

My two children, Victoria and Guy.
And last but not least, the three
little terrors, my wonderful
grandchildren, Madison, Oscar
and Olivia.

Acknowledgements

I'D like to acknowledge those who I had the pleasure of working with over many decades. There are simply too many to mention, but you know who you are.

Sadly Smudger died before the book went to print. My thoughts are with his family.

To my loving family – at least you don't need to read it. You should be word perfect. You have all been great. Thank you.

Thank you to Shaun Esprit, Jo Davis, Alex, Rita and Lorence Zanon, Perry Stewart, Andrew Merriman, John Moore for their diligent editing.

I'd like to say a couple of lines about my ghostwriter. How can you not employ a ghostwriter with a name like Paul Zanon! Our relationship has been one of mutual trust and honesty and I believe we have written a book which fully deserves his signature.

David Beckett, June 2015

Introduction

WHEN I was approached by David Beckett to ghost his life story, I thought to myself, 'What do I know about deep sea diving?' I was genuinely not sure if this was the project for me. Within the first minute of chatting with him, he very calmly asked, 'What experience do you have of diving?' I replied, 'I've gone under with scuba a few times – although not legally.' He calmly responded, 'Not recommended that. How far did you go?' I replied, 'About 18 feet.' Interested in his achievements, I bounced back, 'Give me an idea of how deep you went and what sort of stuff would interest a reader from your life.' He said, 'Over 500 feet – and I've dealt with everything from the salvation of helicopter and ship wreckages, through to being forced to watch public executions. But there's a great deal more to me than just that.' My next comment was, 'You have my undivided attention! Let's meet and write your book.'

On meeting with David, he produced his CV which was 13 pages long. I thought to myself, 'Obviously nobody's told him the protocol of trying to fit a CV on to two pages.' Then I started to read and it became evidently clear why it was 13 pages – in fact, I was impressed with how he had been able to condense it so much. The number of tales to accompany the jobs he completed are only the starter. The script in between the lines of that CV is what you will have the pleasure of reading.

David Beckett is a man of incredible integrity and first and foremost a dedicated family man. He speaks his mind and this book certainly pulls no punches.

Paul Zanon, June 2015

Prelude

*'Forty-five people are feared dead after
a Chinook helicopter carrying oil rig
workers plunged into the North Sea off
the coast of Scotland.'*

(BBC NEWS – 6 November 1986)

W E had just finished a routine deep sea hyperbaric
welding job in the Tartan Field. All I wanted to do was
get to Peterhead and then make my way back to my
loving family. It had been a month, so I was due some R-and-R.

The *Deepwater 1* was a massive robust vessel, but the weather
was so atrocious, it seemed we'd gone backwards ten miles. The
sea coming up underneath the ship's helideck was slamming
so hard, the whole boat was shaking. It genuinely felt like the
helideck was going to come off.

I had a call from the bridge telling me that the operations
manager from the Aberdeen office was on the phone. I knew
something had to be up as he would have never called me for a
social chat.

He told me there'd been a helicopter crash close to the port
of Sumburgh in the Shetlands, and as we were the nearest dive
vessel to its location, there was a good chance we might get a call
from the oil company. They'd also mentioned it was a Chinook.
First thing I thought was, 'That's a big helicopter – which carries
a lot of people. Let's hope it was near empty.'

Sure enough, we got the call. We had already been steaming away for five hours, but changed our course and headed to the site of the accident. At least the waves had calmed down, along with the slamming under the helideck.

A survey vessel was on location within a couple of hours and they had a fish on board – or what is called a Single-beam Scanning Sonar – which was towed behind the boat. It basically mapped the sea bed. If the Chinook could be found before we arrived, we could go straight to the location and start diving.

We arrived in the early hours and they'd not yet detected it, but had just started scanning a new area. The weather was awful. Sixty-miles-per-hour winds and the water temperature was icy cold.

The survival suits they would have been wearing would have given them a few more minutes to survive from the inevitable hyperthermia, but at a little over zero Celsius in choppy waters, it would have literally been a handful of minutes. Forty-seven people had been on board this helicopter and only two survivors had been found. The next 24 to 48 hours were crucial.

Nineteen bodies which had been floating on the surface had already been recovered within six hours of the crash, meaning there were still 26 bodies missing by the time our crew had arrived. Taking into account the dreadful weather conditions we were working under, our instructions were simple – recover as many bodies and wreckage parts as quickly as possible. The reality is that the divers were risking their own lives by getting into those treacherous waters. It was a severe situation on a number of fronts, but we owed it to the families to do our utmost to recover as many bodies as possible.

We didn't know it at the time, but with the number of confirmed dead that were starting to appear, this was about to become one of the biggest civilian helicopter disasters in history. A statistic many would prefer to forget.

Within a couple of hours they called and said they couldn't be sure, but thought their sonar had found a target 300 feet below the surface that could be the Chinook.

I turned to the supervisor and said, 'Tell the divers to get ready. We're going looking for a helicopter.'

The survey vessel had done well to find it at all, as it looked like the Chinook had disintegrated when it hit the water. The largest bit we'd later recover would be an engine.

The big find was the black box as it held essential information as to why this disaster had happened.

The air accident investigation people had sent a couple of guys to the site, who were also joined by a couple of local police officers. The weather had picked up again and the boat was rolling about so badly, that soon after the police helicopter landed, it nearly joined the other one on the sea bed. After that we used wheel chocks.

The diving bell was on the way down to the bottom of the ocean and the investigation guys wanted a meeting with me to establish how I was going to tackle the situation. I explained that I wanted to assess the helicopter and surrounding area before making a decision. This assessment would then reflect the *modus operandi*, i.e. – was the helicopter intact?

It must have been a good plan because they agreed. Although part of me wondered if they agreed in haste because the cops and the investigation team all looked a bit green around the gills. Yup – I think it was seasickness that got them. I hardly saw them again after that meeting.

I got a call from dive control saying the diver had locked out from the bell and was having a look around. Dive control was the best place to be on any diving vessel as it was where all the action happened, so I headed down there straight away. The bridge was the next best place as they always had fresh coffee and biscuits.

The only problem we now faced was a lack of body bags. Before the cops got sick, they said, 'When you recover the bodies will you stick them in body bags?' I replied, 'What body bags?!'

I asked the captain to see if he could come up with a solution. He was working on it – all night as it would turn out.

Back in dive control, a couple of guys were looking at the pictures from the ROV (Remotely Operated underwater Vehicle) and the diver's hat-mounted camera, when out of the blue, bouncing across the sea bed were two bodies still strapped into their seats. We'd found the Chinook.

It was still early days and we weren't fully ready for body recovery but I told the deck to send the cargo net down on the whip line of the crane. They soon had the cargo net down to the diver ready to load up with bodies.

I'd been talking to the captain who had found some giant bin liners. They didn't have zips or anything like the real thing but would do for now. We had no choice.

When I got back to dive control things weren't going as planned. The diver was trying to wrestle one of the bodies into the cargo net which kept trying to float away, while using one of his legs to keep the net in place.

I did say we weren't quite ready.

In the end, we made up four stakes and pinned the net to the sea bed. I asked the deck to send the steel net down next time. I thought it might make life a bit easier for the diver with the extra weight – and it did. Unfortunately, the steel nets would eventually come with their own problems.

With the heavier net in place, the diver managed to get the two lads into it, and we were ready to recover them to the surface. They may have been dead, but it was essential for me to ensure these guys surfaced with some dignity. Remembering the decompression rules, I told the crane driver to bring them up slowly – however, later I found out it didn't matter, because everyone was wearing their survival suits and if anyone had already blown their lungs or were about to, nobody would have been able to see.

The fact that the crew on board the helicopter were wearing their safety belts certainly helped in terms of identification, more than anything, because the belts kept them in their seat as opposed to allowing them to float off into the ocean. At that point there was no guarantee of recovering their bodies.

It was weird seeing them bobbing about, still sat in their seats with their hoods up. We arrived about 24 hours after the crash and a lot can happen underwater during that time. By the look of their faces they'd stopped dead or the marine life had been quick to start eating away at them. It wasn't pretty.

The other problem we faced involved the news people who'd heard about the tragedy and had a helicopter flying around. Rumour was, Kate Adie was out drifting around in a boat trying to get an exclusive. I understood the media had a job to do, but so did I. More importantly, sons, husbands and brothers had died out there, and I felt like they deserved some discretion.

I didn't want to bring the net up in view of the helicopter. I thought that might be insensitive so I waited until the helicopter was a good way away then told the crane driver to bring the bodies on board. It was a good job I did because as soon as the net was pulled on board, the seagulls swooped and started pecking away at the human flesh. They always used to hang around the ships and rigs, hoping there was a few fish to scavenge. It was a truly awful sight to witness.

They were like vultures those things. No shooing away or shouting made a difference, so it was up and on as quick as the crane driver could go. Once we had the bodies on the deck we put a shelter over them, so no prying helicopter could take pictures.

You might have expected the cops to give us a hand getting the bodies into the bags, but they were nowhere to be seen. They were struggling with seasickness so this task would have broken them.

We needed four people to ensure a body was correctly put into a bag and the reality was, we were short of hands.

There was no way I could get them in the bag on my own, so it was volunteer time. Life support technicians, any divers hanging about, basically anyone willing to help.

The front two put their foot and left hand on the bag – the foot to hold it down and the hand to keep it open. The other two would help slide the body into the bag. The system was simple: one, two, three, *in*. As it worked well, we stuck with this system for all of the bodies.

However, despite all the best will in the world, the volunteers did struggle with what was a very challenging task of having to physically handle bodies which were missing flesh and which were frozen in shape. It was frightening, but what was about to happen would mentally scar even the toughest of people.

It happened, on reaching 'two' in our system, when the head of one of the bodies fell off and bounced on to the deck. The wet sound it made on hitting the deck was sickening and to see parts of the head fall out was awful.

I thought to myself, 'Fuck me. What else has today got in store for us?' At that precise moment, I heard what sounded like a heavy sack of cement being dropped on the deck next to me. One of the volunteers who'd bravely stepped forward to help had just fainted. Volunteers were thin on the ground to start with, but they started to become even more scarce now.

After this happened, I made them put the bodies face down as it was easier to assist the volunteer with the whole process of handling a dead person. The bags did the job, although the feet stuck out. Given our resources and the circumstances, it was as good as we could do.

The divers were now finding bodies thick and fast and were ready for the next net. This time we sent the steel net down. When you start to find a mass of bodies, you need to detach yourself emotionally. It sounds awful, and although it may seem insensitive, especially to any families reading this who may have lost a loved one on that helicopter, my aim was first and foremost to recover those bodies and do so in a manner which was fast, out of the public eye and in the most dignified way possible with the limited resources we had.

Finally, it looked like we'd cracked it. The net stayed flat on the sea bed and the diver soon had it filled again with five poor lads. This time we were ready. On the deck we'd use the same routine with the helicopter and seagulls. Up they came on to the deck, quick as you like.

It wasn't until we opened the net that it became obvious the steel net had been cutting into their faces and leaving square marks.

'We can't send them home with squares on their faces,' I thought. I decided we'd have to go back to using the rope net and the stakes. It was slower but I figured these divers had plenty of time and we were on a day rate – most importantly, in the long run the bodies would be brought to the deck in far better condition.

Working around the clock, I dealt with every net that came up. We had lights pointing at the area of the ocean where the nets would rise and each time a new net surfaced we all took a gulp of air for what to potentially expect. At one point I remember one of the volunteers looking at their watch and it was 2am. I remember saying to him, 'I know we've been working non-stop for a day and it's not fair, but I really appreciate your help.' But what did 'fair' have to do with anything? All you had to do was look at the lads in the net – that was not fair.

Keeping focused was essential. Being emotional would put the task in hand in jeopardy. It's the equivalent of a paramedic turning up to the scene of a car wreck and having to deal with somebody's shin bone sticking out of their leg and bodies everywhere. Person X has an injury of Y, and Z is the solution. Stop for a second to drop a tear at the overall situation and they lose focus of the task in hand. I was in a similar situation. I needed to be as efficient as possible, with the ultimate task of recovering each and every body.

The news helicopter that was flying around was a nuisance. So I decided to play a trick on them. I got three of the lads to put survival suits on and when the helicopter was away, I told them to lay at the stern of the boat, side by side, and not to move until I told them. When the helicopter did appear again, I told them to jump up and down and wave. It never appeared on the news, but it did lighten the atmosphere on the boat. Even the cops laughed…before going back to the toilets to throw up.

In between nets, I'd go into the TV lounge to see what they were saying about the salvage operation on the news. If memory serves me correctly, Trevor McDonald (now Sir Trevor) was describing the situation here on deck. I'm a big fan of Trevor, but I often wondered if I was on the same job that he was talking about.

Whenever there is an aviation disaster and it hits the television, an 'expert' always pops up to give their theories. It tends to be a retired pilot.

The expert on this occasion who was advising the television broadcasters was way off. The reason would surface later that it was a gearbox issue – simple as that.

It was strange to watch a news report about a job I was on. I wondered who they were getting their facts from. It also made me wonder about other news stories and their validity, as there were suddenly more experts and opinions than facts. But we all know what they say about opinions: they're like backsides – everyone has one.

While looking for survivors, I realised it didn't take much of an 'expert' to explain that several people in a helicopter who crashed into the North Sea and had since been laid there for 36 hours, didn't have much of a chance of surviving – especially as there are no air pockets at 300 feet below the surface. Being paid a fat wad, while sat in a nice warm studio together with a good imagination, it would be easy to find a nice little air pocket that could keep someone alive.

I'm sure there were one or two media guys who had good intentions, but this lot infuriated me with their commentary.

We must have pulled out six or seven nets full of dead bodies. Don't let anyone tell you that each net becomes easier to look at – it doesn't. These guys, a matter of hours ago, had a life. They would have been excited about going home, as they'd have just finished their two-week stint working offshore and were probably looking forward to two weeks off.

They would have watched the survival video and got into their survival suits, not knowing it was for the last time, selected a magazine to read on the flight or saved the last few pages of a book they'd been reading. There would have been a quick call to a loved one to say the helicopter was on time and that they'd be on it and, all being well, home that night.

The helicopter would have taken them from the rig to Sumburgh, where they would have then caught a fixed wing to Aberdeen, then onward to wherever their loved ones were waiting. They all belonged to someone.

Now, they were in makeshift body bags, in a rigger's container on the back of a diving vessel.

I wondered about their mothers, wives, children, girlfriends, perhaps their boyfriends. What of their lives? I wondered what it would be like for those mothers trying to explain that 'dad's never coming home again'; to cancel a wedding as the groom had been lost to the sea; a mother and father's grief of losing their only child. It was easy to be carried away with such thoughts. I expect most of them expected the worst when they saw the news bulletins.

Up to this point in my life, I didn't have a great deal of experience of touching dead bodies, due to wearing my diving equipment, which took the sensitivity out of the experience. This time it was far more poignant due to my skin making contact with the skin of a dead body.

As we didn't have a proper container to put the bodies in, I had them clean out the rigger's container and use that instead. It wasn't refrigerated but it was cold enough. By the end though, it wasn't very pleasant.

Next up was the remains of the cockpit. The co-pilot came up still holding the joystick, with a big hole in his head. As a result of rigor mortis, it took quite an effort to make him release that joystick. The poor man must have honourably been trying to control the helicopter right to the very end.

After about 48 hours we were given instructions to stop the search for bodies. I believe the balance of those missing had now been accounted for, which at least allowed me to feel some relief for their relatives.

In terms of the two survivors, they were incredibly lucky. The BBC reported that both had been rescued from the freezing water – one was found hanging on to a piece of floating wreckage and the other was hanging on to a dinghy.

However, our work was not done yet.

We immediately started to retrieve the helicopter remains – bit by bit it came up, covered in seaweed, mud and silt, while being blown around by the wind at sea while on the crane. The wreckage salvation process all went fine – apart from the rotor blades that was. On trying to recover them, it very quickly became obvious just how ungainly they were. With the crane nearly as high as it could reach and the rotors hanging down, it just about cleared the sides of the boat. The crane driver started swinging the load on board and the whole thing started slashing across the deck before he could get it down.

Hydraulic cranes are not the fastest cranes in the world and all the blades were hanging down, going across the deck like a giant scythe. At one point I had to jump up and let the blade go under my feet. They're a lot longer than they look and I must have been standing too close. Lesson learned.

Most of the pieces of the helicopter went into the skip and back to Aberdeen after the air investigators had taken pictures. I was glad to see the back of the craft, as I'm sure many of the loved ones close to those who had perished would have most likely agreed.

We did get a visit from the procurator fiscal (public prosecutor) soon after we had retrieved the bodies. He was quite high up in the Scottish system and I guess it was important he showed his face. That's about all he did though. I guess if you've never landed on a helipad which is heaving up and down with gale force winds blowing at you, it could feel scary. It sure must have scared him as minutes later he was gone.

We handled almost everything before the oil company's vessel arrived to take over. They lifted everything off our deck, including the container. I remember thinking, respectfully, 'I wouldn't like to be the man who opened that.'

The whole operation took about three days. We pinched any time in between nets to grab some sleep, but it wouldn't be a lie to say we were totally exhausted by the end. I picked up a nickname after this job which was one I was glad to lose over time – 'Body Bag Beckett'.

Unfortunately, the future would hold further hairy episodes in store for me. That said, my past was hardly uneventful.

1

David Harrison Beckett

I WAS born on 1 June 1947 in Tuddenham, Suffolk. The Beckett family lived like nomads during those early years, so I can't really claim I was bred there.

My father was a squadron leader in the RAF, piloting Hurricanes and Spitfires, squirting down 109s (Messerschmitts) during World War II in Malta. My mother was also in the RAF, but in all honesty I'm not really sure what her role was. Anyway – I'm guessing they met in the RAF, as I never really asked.

Soon after the war my dad left the RAF, but jobs were scarce, so he decided to go straight back to them, initially flying, but eventually working crash investigation for bomber command.

As a result of him being in the forces for 25 years, my siblings and I grew up all over the place. As a kid I thought it was normal to constantly be on the move – I didn't know any different. However, I do look back at those times with a smile as I have some fond memories of the adventures we embarked on.

At the ripe old age of five, we headed off to the bush in Australia. The Suez Canal had just about been cleaned and cleared after the war, so we left the UK and headed through on the RMS *Strathnaver*. As you crossed the equator, old father time would crawl up on to the boat and give you a certificate confirming that you had officially made the crossing. Well that's what they told me. Several weeks later we arrived in Oz.

I don't remember a great deal about my time Down Under, but three memories certainly stand out. Firstly, the time when the school was on fire and we all had to run into the sea to be safe, and secondly was walking to school through the bush and standing on a massive snake. The snake slithered off in one direction and I hardly touched the ground as I sprinted off to school.

My third memory was swimming. At the time, my dad used to play water polo for the RAF and was a very proficient swimmer, so he started teaching me. Within a few weeks I did my 25-yard swimming test in the sea and passed. Little did I know as a six-year-old that this was an early induction into a substance that I would be deeply involved in for three decades.

My next memory was coming back to the UK on the SS *Orcades*. Neither ship exists anymore. The *Strathnaver* was scrapped in 1962 in Hong Kong and the *Orcades* ten years later in Taiwan.

Aged seven, we moved back to the UK to Hemsby, but for the next few years we moved about a fair bit within the Norfolk and Suffolk boundaries, and by the age of eight, I had already attended seven different schools. I'm not sure if that contributed to my lack of enthusiasm for school, or if I was just never destined to be an academic.

I failed pretty much everything, so that ruled out technical college. I used to get zero out of 30 for spelling and failed the 11 Plus. I was already heavily dyslexic at this point, but in the 1950s, if you were dyslexic, you were simply branded as not being very able on the reading and writing front. I did however come top in the pigs module in my City and Guilds qualification a few years later at agricultural college. What an honour.

The thing is, I didn't really have a major ambition to become a farmer – it was kind of a natural progression from the environment I was in. At the time I was living on a farm and thought, 'I might as well be a farmer. What else is out there for me?'

2

Becoming A
Bubble Head

I'VE often been asked how I became a deep sea diver and threw
away the opportunity to become a pig farmer, especially after
I'd passed my tractor driving test when I was only 16.

My route to diving was not a conventional one. As opposed
to many who entered a diving career following a grounding in
the military, I wasn't even a former pig farmer at this stage. I was
in essence a kid looking to land his first job to pay the bills as a
result of getting kicked out of the house.

My parents had gone away for a couple of days so I thought,
like you do when you're 20, 'Let's have a party!' Seemed like a
good idea at the time. What could possibly go wrong?

Thing is, word had got about – *really* got about. Everyone I
had invited brought a friend or eight and without trying to lose
my cool reputation as a guy who had organised a great house
party, I let everyone in.

In those days, where I came from, when you went to a party
you took along a barrel of beer. At the time it was Watneys Red
Barrel which contained about five or six pints of bitter and, would
you believe it, came in a red tin barrel.

I won't go into the ins and outs of what happened at the party.
Suffice to say, every bed was used, the house was unintentionally

redecorated and the need for a very challenging clear-up was evident.

I was only thinking of my dad when I filled the big double door fridge up with the half-empty tins of beer. He liked his beer and used to make his own, which in all honesty tasted like shit, so I thought I was doing him a favour leaving him a load of Red Barrel.

I did the best I could with the clean-up operation, but when you're only 20 years old you can't do it as well as your mum. I didn't even know how to work the washing machine, let alone make the beds properly. I didn't cover my tracks very well.

They arrived home that evening and in under three minutes I was busted. Dad opened the fridge, only to be hit with a sea of Red Barrel, which started off a non-stop shouting marathon directed my way, insisting first and foremost I put his home brew back. No wonder they grounded him when he was in the air force – he must have been unstable even in those days. Although, looking back I can understand the genesis of his anger.

Mum and dad agreed it was high time I found new digs. That kind of signified the end of my childhood and later that night I was looking for somewhere to stay. I guess I had to leave one day. It was goodbye to home cooking, clean laundry, having my bed made, free electricity and use of the phone. I didn't miss dad's beer though.

With a bag over my shoulder, I eventually found a boarding house that had a room. It was late by this time and I was ready for bed. The landlady showed me my room and told me what time breakfast was. She made me pay a deposit up front. I remember thinking she wasn't like my mum – I used to give her an IOU.

I said thanks, shut the door, got undressed, jumped into bed and nearly skidded straight out the other side with sparks flying from where my bum was getting electric shocks. It turned out the sheets were made of nylon. If you've ever slept on nylon sheets, you'll know what I mean.

The following morning at breakfast, the table next to me had some rough-looking dudes sitting on it who were giving me the once over. One of them asked me if I was going out with them. What sort of place was this, I wondered? I think I blushed.

The conversation was a bit confusing but it turned out that they weren't proposing to me – they wanted to know if I was the diver they were waiting for. It seems they all worked for a company called Delta Diving and stayed at this boarding house the night before they went offshore.

We got chatting and it seemed like a well-paid job. One of the divers hadn't turned up so they were one short. He said, 'If you've got nothing else to do, why not come with us?' There was no job spec, but they said they'd train me on the job. I could swim, but I knew absolutely nothing about diving.

I'd just finished my agricultural course which had entailed three years of hard work. At that point in my life I'd pretty much decided I was going to become a farm manager with a tweed jacket, driving round in a Land Rover chewing a piece of straw, that sort of thing. I thought about it for a moment, before saying to the lads, 'Why not?' And with that, I packed my bags.

Before heading off on my maiden voyage, I needed to pass a medical. In those days you only needed a blue book with a doctor's note saying you were fit to dive.

In order to get that note though, the doc gave me a strict medical in which he checked almost every part of me starting with my old jam tart. You had to lay down and get all these suction pads put on with cold jelly, then they checked my heart rate to make sure everything was okay.

The first bit was fine, then I climbed off the bed and jumped up and down on a step about a foot high 30 times per minute for five minutes. I was allowed to change the step leg halfway through. After five minutes of this my heart was thumping away like mad. They didn't need a machine to hear mine but I think they liked the machine to draw a graph. This test showed how fit I was – or not.

I'm surprised no one ever had a heart attack.

The doctor said, 'We also like to x-ray your long bones to see how much decompression could cause your bones to crumble in later life.' Decompression? What was that? A few baptisms of fire would turn me into a micro-expert on the subject down the line.

Once you'd done your medical you could assume you were fairly fit. You needed to do one, because when it came to diving, it was the equivalent of your diving licence.

The final part was always bemusing. I never did understand why they held your testicles and asked you to cough – and yes this did actually happen.

After the medical was finished, he stamped the blue book and up to the heliport we went.

On arrival, I phoned mum and dad to tell them I'd had a career change. My dad had been a pilot in the war so I think he liked the idea of me becoming a deep sea diver, as it had a strong element of discipline to it. He hated farmers, for which he had his reasons – namely because one had been sleeping with my mother while my dad was away flying for the RAF.

The guy who came to pick the divers up was the equivalent of a modern day operations manager. He used to be the road manager for the band Manfred Mann. No idea what that's got to do with diving, but there you go.

He didn't object when the guys told him I was going with them and that they'd train me on the job. He told me how much I would get paid. The other lads got the day rate raised a bit for me and it ended up being £14 a day. I didn't get that per week working on the farm, not even with eight hours of overtime. I was a happy bunny.

I'd never been in a helicopter before and I was the youngest of the crew. Act brave, I thought.

You'd grab a seat and put your kit bag next to you. If you were the one near the door you would put a sort of leather thing on your head with something that went around your throat. It turned out to be a throat microphone so you could talk to the pilot – he needed to know when the door was shut and everyone was ready for take-off.

Start-up was fun. It was shake, rattle, and roll as this thing attempted to lift off the ground. It did all sorts of dipping and shaking before the pilot eventually got the thing level. Then he seemed to go straight up, dipped the nose and away we went over the cliffs and out to sea.

It was only a 25-minute flight out to the rig. As we approached the helideck, I thought to myself, 'Are you kidding me?? Surely we're not landing on that little thing?' I would have preferred a much bigger target, but nobody else seemed concerned, so I kept my trap shut. After all, I was now a deep sea diver…albeit one who'd never been underwater before.

Landing in the helicopter was the best bit. With a lot of shaking, the pilot seemed to come to a stop above the helideck, hovered to one side, stayed there for a few minutes, then very slowly, slipped sideways over the deck and down with a thud. We'd landed.

The pilot left the rotor turning so when the man came to open the door, he was bent right over to avoid getting his head cut off. I remember thinking, 'I'm going to do that,' as I wanted to see if I could make it to my first pay day. It was all a bit scary this career change, but things were just about to get a whole lot scarier.

I got out of the helicopter remembering to keep my head down, but nearly got blown away as I wasn't expecting the wind coming across the helideck. That would have been a great start – the other divers jumping in to save me. The guys seemed to be doing okay, so I stayed low and followed them down into the helicopter arrival room.

This was the place they took your name and allocated you to a cabin. It turned out to be a big cabin with about ten bunks in it, which were stacked five high, with a ladder at the end. I was allocated a locker for my kit, and thankfully a bunk which didn't have nylon sheets. Already a step up from the boarding house.

It was starting to look like these rigs were built for work, not comfort. Communal showers I could handle, as I used to sit in a big bath drinking beer after a rugby match. However, the toilet situation was a bit trickier, as they didn't have doors. I went in and made sure no one else was in there and tried to do it as quickly as possible – it never seemed to work out though.

One day this big American walked in, unclasped his dungarees, pulled down these enormous pair of boxer shorts, and plopped himself down next to me. I think he wanted a bit of company. Well, next thing there was an almighty fart and it was all over. A quick wipe and it was back up with the boxers and dungarees. He looked at me and winked. As he left he said, 'That's the way to do it,' before continuing with, 'Don't worry, boy. You've got beginner's nerves.'

I remember thinking he must have eaten a lot of sprouts. We soon became friendly and often sat together. I think I was even quicker than him one day.

It was a good learning curve as, later on, when I became a saturation diver they'd watch your every move on the TV. Or perhaps that's every 'movement'.

Back to my first day on the job.

The mess room was good as was the standard of food. I could pretty much eat all day if I wanted, which as a 20-year-old with unlimited appetite was perfect. Steak and chips four times – why not? However, as opposed to home life, these rigs were dry. Strictly no alcohol. I was apparently now a responsible working adult.

The time had come to work. The lads had a chat with the tool pusher, who was in charge of things and told us what to do. He wanted us to go down each leg of the rig in turn and check for scouring.

The guys explained to me, because of the strong tides in the North Sea, when the rigs spudded inwards, it would push each leg down as far as they would go, which in turn would then flood the bottom chamber. However, the sand around the bottom could get washed away and the rig could become unstable. If this looked like it was going to happen they'd bring boatloads of sandbags out and lower them down for us divers to place around the legs. Seemed fairly straightforward. In fact, just like humping bags of spuds about. I knew my training would come in handy one day!

The next step was to show me how we would get down there. One of the guys called Albert showed me the equipment and how it worked. Albert was from London and used to be a getaway driver – until he stalled. He did a bit of time and somehow became a diver. I must say, he was a lovely chap and a very big help.

First thing he showed me was the rubber wetsuit, which was made from very thick rubber. He said the thicker the better as it would help keep me warm. Sounded good to me.

Next up was the Desco diving mask, which had a hose that went to the surface air compressor on the top deck. The mask was a constant pressure mask, which meant the air was forced into it. All I had to do was open my mouth and breathe. Inside the mask was a little round microphone stuck on the glass with putty. This hi-tech piece of equipment was the communications (aka 'comms') to the surface.

Albert said, 'When you're underwater, the air rushing around inside the mask will make so much noise, you won't hear anything from the comms. You'll just feel a little vibration on your nose.' My first thought was, 'Aren't I the lucky one with a larger than average nose.' The way to make it work was to turn off the air to the mask and try and be as quiet as possible. I really had to concentrate to hear anything but it did work. Although, the first time I was a bit reluctant to turn the air off.

Next, I was given a weight belt to make me sink, as rubber suits were buoyant – which did come in handy now and again, as you will read later. Lastly, I had a pair of fins which were called 'AP', which stood for Admiral Pattern. I stuffed my feet in these and pulled a strap up round the back of my heel.

With all the kit on, I couldn't wait to get going.

I didn't have to wait long as the next day was initiation day. Once we arrived at the changing room, I struggled to get into the wetsuit. Thankfully the lads saw me wrestling around with it and told me to use talcum powder next time as it would help me slide straight in. And it did!

Another trick was to wear a pair of ladies' tights. Some of the guys used to wear stockings. Whatever turns you on I guess.

Once the suit was on, I waddled off to the lower deck, then down to the boat landing which was about 30 feet above the sea. The masks and everything else were down there, coiled up and ready to go. Less than 48 hours after eating breakfast at the boarding house I was moments away from diving.

It was me and Albert on this day. I looked down and asked Albert how we were going to get into the water. I shouldn't have as it was simple really.

'Jump,' he said.

When I looked down again it seemed further. I looked at him and he just nodded. I already had my diver's knife on, so it was on with the AP fins and weight belt. I was beginning to feel the part. Up with the hood and on with the mask. Albert said he'd go first and wait for me just below the splash zone. I later found out this was about 30 feet down. It's where you lose the effect of the surface swell.

Albert was gone. Hands holding his mask, fins crossed and pointed down just like they told me to do it. The guy on the surface threw enough umbilical over the side so I'd go straight down once I hit the water. He gave me the nod and I jumped.

When I hit the water I must have forgotten everything they'd taught me. The mask came up and nearly broke my nose – in fact, the only reason I think it stayed on was because of the size of it.

I was flapping my feet to try and get some kind of orientation, bubbles were everywhere, and there was what seemed like a roaring noise going through my mask. My flippers weren't working and, to put it mildly, nor was my brain.

I felt a tug on my arm and there was good old Albert, pulling me down to the nearest bracing.

Once he got me under control I could see he was killing himself laughing. My fins were up around my knees, but thankfully he pulled them down for me – by which time I was finally getting orientated and my breathing was okay. I could even see things around me. The rig underwater looked the same as it did above the water, just like the lads said it would.

Time was of the essence in the southern sector of the North Sea. You only had four slack tides a day, so you had to get on with things. Albert pointed down and started going down the leg into what looked like the gloom. My ears really started hurting and I remembered what the lads had told me: swallow or yawn until you felt them pop. Swallow worked for me and down we went. I loved eating mussels and there were millions of them on the rig leg, although you couldn't eat these as they'd grown on metal. The further I went down, the quieter and more crackly it became. The bottom was around 80 feet, which for a first dive was pretty deep. It appeared fairly suddenly and I was surprised how much I could see. There were crabs walking about together with cod and all kinds of other fish swimming around.

Marine life apart, the sea bed was a mess. There must have been 50 scaffold poles laying around, lumps of steel, and all sorts of debris. It looked like a scene from the movie *Zulu*, with Michael Caine and those tall African warriors slinging spears.

Albert was doing what we were meant to be doing while I was still in shock. I do remember thinking I should be helping him.

He was pointing at my mask and making a motion to turn off my valve, but there was no way I was going to touch that let alone turn off my air supply. There's no way I could tell if the end of my nose was tingling with someone trying to talk to me. It was still throbbing from when I had hit the water. I did manage to follow Albert about, but didn't achieve anything work wise.

I started to feel the water move – the tide was picking up. I got the sign to head back up. Halfway up I thought, 'How do we get out?' I then remembered them saying there was a ladder going up to the boat landing, but hadn't bothered to look.

It was coming back, what they'd told me, 'You get hold of the bottom rung of the ladder, take your fins off, put them over your wrists, and climb the ladder.' In reality, what happened was, you got hold of the bottom of the ladder, then the next minute the swell lifted you halfway up the ladder then down again. It turned out to be tricky and I was lucky not to hurt myself.

After a few times doing this, I learnt how to use the swell to my advantage. If you timed it right you'd get hold of the ladder at the top of the swell and hold on for all you were worth until the swell had gone down, then climb like crazy before the next wave hit you. Doing this, you'd eliminate half of the 30-foot climb.

When I got back, that first time, my legs were like jelly and I was completely knackered. After a while it did get easier and became a lot more fun.

I didn't realise it at the time, but I was about to embark on a lifelong career and join a long line of individuals looking to explore, search for food, salvage and repair underwater. The latter being what I would be doing for many years to come.

I was now a commercial diver, albeit a very green one, which stemmed from a history dating back as far as the 1800s, when the industrial revolution was in full flow. Everybody wanted to build a tunnel, a bridge or a pier back then, so as a result many people ended up immersed in water at some point.

Even the equipment hadn't changed a great deal in the last couple of hundred years. Diving bells and suits were similar, it's just that technology combined with scientific research had brought them forward leaps and bounds. Understanding pressurised air and the safe levels of ascent after being in a pressurised environment, buoyancy, and the influence and correct mixtures of air, helium and gas did not happen overnight. A steep learning curve awaited me. Many divers perished to help the likes of myself have this knowledge and in the years ahead of me, the same would happen again, with those disasters assisting future generations. The only downside is that I would be involved in witnessing some of those disasters.

At this moment in time, I was air diving. I was officially a bubble head. Although I thought I was deep at 80 feet, the seriously deep stuff awaited me a few years ahead. For now, I was either working with an umbilical or with a 'self contained underwater breathing apparatus'. You may know this as SCUBA. Originally the invention of Jacques Cousteau and Emile Gagnan, and referred to by the English for many years as the 'Aqua-lung', SCUBA revolutionised diving.

When I left the surface of the water, it was almost as if I metamorphosed into another creature. It's almost like I ceased to be a human being and turned into a new species called 'A Diver'.

I was not a fish or aquatic mammal, but as with both of these, I now operated in a certain way underwater. Totally differently to the way I did on land.

As I reflected on my first stint as a diver, my change of career was completed with my first pay day.

I had never been so rich – on a number of levels.

3

No Air

GETTING to grips with the tides as an air diver was probably the toughest part of my job in the early days. In the end, I followed a tried and tested technique developed by the other divers, which worked.

I always used to take a piece of rope to tie myself to the work site. It meant I had two hands to work with instead of hanging on with one hand and trying to do whatever job I was doing with the other. Unfortunately, this technique came with its downsides.

One day in 1968, I was happily working away at around 120 feet when the air went off. We used the air supplied by the rig's compressor. It was just a standard air compressor which they used for tuggers and deck tools. We would run it through a deltec filter which took all the impurities out of it – this was on the boat landing far removed from the deck compressor which was on the main deck.

While diving we'd hang a sign on the compressor saying, 'Please don't turn off – there are divers working down below who are using this air.' Though it never seemed to stop some of those roustabouts turning the thing off.

You're never prepared for the air to go off but, believe me, it never goes off when you've just breathed in, only when you've just unloaded your lungs. You normally hear a click as something shuts behind your head signalling there's no more air available. The thing is not to panic.

Panic kills, that's what they told me in training. It's good advice.

Many people react by taking their air piece out of their mouth, thinking, 'It doesn't have any air, it's no use to me now,' but you need to keep it in and concentrate on coming up. Taking it out will put you in jeopardy.

Air diving is different to saturation diving. You can come up when you're air diving, so long as you hadn't gone beyond your 'free time' (the allocated time underwater at depth before needing decompression).

The golden rule as an air diver is to follow the bubbles. You don't go up any faster than the bubbles you breathe out. When they taught Navy people to do an escape from a submarine, they did it in a deep vertical tank and there was an instructor halfway up. If the instructor saw you were not blowing out air, he would hit you hard, in order to make you blow out. Option B is to retain the air and let your lungs literally explode as you start to ascend.

So, when I heard the click that day I thought, 'That's it – I'm heading for the surface rapido.' To hell with the golden rule about the bubbles.

I dropped my weight belt and anything else that didn't float and headed upwards. I'd gone about ten feet and was looking up to the surface accelerating as fast as my flippers could take me to my air supply. It's the same equivalent of needing to go to the loo for a pee and the nearer you get, the more you anticipate the end result.

Gathering speed, I could almost taste the fresh air above when I came to a sudden jerking holt. As I lost more of what little air was left in my lungs, for the second time in a matter of seconds I was having to remind myself, 'Panic kills.'

I then thought, 'Shit, what's happened now?!' I realised I was still tied to the bottom of the ocean.

Divers' knives look like fearsome weapons but are actually as blunt and cumbersome as can be. On this particular day, I pulled myself back down and sliced that piece of rope like I had a razor blade in my hand. You always find a little bit more strength when you need it.

Up I went again, leaving the knife at the bottom of the ocean, with my arms over my head in case I hit a bracing on the ascent. Although I had no air left by this time, as I went up faster and faster, I became more buoyant. Although I couldn't feel it, the air in my lungs was doubling in that last 30 feet. If I had held my breath, my lungs would have exploded and that would have been the end of a promising diving career. Believe me, you have to blow like crazy to get it out quick enough. You're better off drinking water for the last 30 feet than having any left when you get to the surface. I drunk my fair share on this occasion.

As I reached the surface, I popped right out. The same equivalent of holding a football under the water and letting it go. It must have looked quite strange to anyone who had seen me from a passing boat or looking down from the rig. That said, I couldn't care less how stupid I looked, as I'd just stared death in the face for the first time – but certainly not the last.

4

Blowout

IN those days you didn't stay on the same rig for long. They only wanted you when there was a specific job and were glad to see the back of us as soon as possible. We used to eat way too much. We were always first in the mess room and had the best seats in the TV lounge.

Talking of TV lounges, during my first few months as a diver I was watching a cowboy movie on another rig when – BANG – the TV fell off the shelf on the wall and shattered, as the whole rig shuddered. I ran to the window to see mud spurting out of the drill floor. I thought we were about to blow up. I was hoping not, as I'd only had seven pay cheques and thought I'd already had enough drama for such a short diving career to date.

The weather that Sunday was blowing a hooley and the sea was particularly rough. In the emergency briefings they told us we would have a lifeboat to go to, failing that, we would go down the scrambling nets with our life jacket on and jump in.

I looked out of the door but saw no activity around the lifeboats. There was no way I was going down the scramble nets into the water – it was rough as a bastard. I wouldn't have lasted two minutes in that sea.

I headed up to the helideck just as a helicopter was landing. As it landed, they waved me over and indicated I opened the door and got in. I put the leather hat on and throat microphone round my neck. The pilot asked if there was anyone else coming.

I said I didn't know as I was first out the door after I'd heard the bang.

'What shall we do?' he said.

'Take off,' I replied. And with that, he did.

We landed on a rig nearby. Turned out they'd seen all the mud coming out of the drilling derrick and notified the powers that be that there was a problem.

I got out of the helicopter and told them what little I knew. They were a little surprised that I was on my own. I did stress there always has to be one survivor to tell the tale.

They sent the helicopter back several times for more survivors. I was lucky really, as the helicopter was passing on his way to another rig when he saw the mud coming out of the rig's derrick and decided to land.

Later that day we were flown ashore and taken by the local press to the Three Bears pub in Great Yarmouth and given ten bob and a pint of Red Barrel to tell our story. I didn't give them much of a story for ten bob and a pint. I also lost all my clothes that I'd left behind, including my best corduroy shirt.

Later that week they flew a man out who worked for Red Adair – the most famous person in the oil industry. The guy was called Boots Hansen. He soon sorted things out – rumour has it he dropped three marbles down the offending pipe which did the trick and stopped the mud spurting out.

He didn't find my shirt, though.

No one was reported as being injured which I was glad to hear. I continued to work with Albert for a year or so. He was a good guy to be around. A lot different to the farmer boys I was used to, that's for sure. His education didn't just stop at diving though.

5

Learning All
The Time

IT was around this time I learned a very valuable lesson. I still have the scars to prove it. We were in a pub in Great Yarmouth called, would you believe it, The Divers. We were having a drink when this lad walked up to me and asked me why I was looking at his girlfriend. I say 'lad', but he looked about the same age as me – 20 years old or so.

Being a deep sea diver and quickly becoming a smart arse I said, 'You've got the wrong person – I never look at ugly women.'

You'd have thought I'd just kicked him in the nuts. I actually wish I had.

'You and me, outside,' he said.

'Might as well,' I thought. So off I went without thinking to tell the other lads. As soon as I got out the door I realised my mistake, as all his mates were waiting. I legged it as fast as I could go. I tell you, Steve McQueen had nothing on me – it was *The Great Escape, Part II*.

I must have made 20 yards on them when I thought I'd turn right down an alley, right again, right again, and I'd be back at the pub door. It was a good plan until I came out of the alley when wham, bam, thank you ma'am! Half his mates had gone down the other side. I couldn't help thinking they'd done this before. Last thing I remember is looking up at a big cherry-red Dr Marten fast coming my way.

When I woke up, Albert, who'd taken me to A and E, said, 'Let that be a lesson to you. Never go outside – do it there and then as they won't be expecting it.'

Thanks Albert.

That was my first good kicking and thankfully my last. Lesson learnt.

Albert and I parted company after a job in Ireland. We were working on an oil tanker terminal in Bantry Bay. It was relatively new and we were finishing it, cutting bits off, and doing a bit of underwater painting. If you think changing a nappy is messy, try underwater painting.

Painting was right in the splash zone and to get the paint to stick on the legs of this terminal you had to go very slow with the brush to allow the heat of the paint to push the water out of the way and bond itself to the metal. Well, that was the theory. In reality it didn't work. You would complete the brushstroke, slowly remove the brush, then watch the paint roll all the way down and disperse into the water, covering you during the process.

We tried everything to stop the paint getting inside our diving suits and on to our skin. It used to burn, bring you out in a rash and no matter what you did, it always managed to get you. Washing yourself in turps would get it off, so long as you made sure you didn't smoke afterwards.

One night, a big Japanese oil tanker moored at our work location. You could see the hull clearly from our worksite. I knew we shouldn't have done it, but we thought the tanker was loading and would be off soon. Over we went like underwater saboteurs with our paint, and in big grey letters wrote 'ASO' on the hull. It did show a lack of maturity but we thought it would wash off on the way back to Japan or, better still, not stick like it had a habit of doing.

The next day was not good. The tanker had been de-ballasting and was completely out of the water. For once the paint had stuck. 'ASO' was all you could see. As we were the only divers out there underwater, it didn't take them long to figure out the culprits. Painting the tanker was certainly quicker than it was scrubbing it off – which for the record took five hours.

We received a reprimand from the terminal boss. Honestly, no sense of humour.

We operated off a local work barge called the *Bernadette*. It was crewed by a nice local Irish family (or so we thought), who we got on well with. They'd do the tea and coffee and we'd dive down to the bottom of the sea and pick up a sack of scallops and the odd lobster for lunch. They'd have a big pan of boiling water bubbling away ready to put them in, and some nice fresh bread with Irish butter. It was a lunch fit for the gods.

One day, one of the crew told us he'd been approached by some lads asking what we were doing. He'd told them, but the lads said that the local people could do the same work. In other words, we were taking their work away. The thing was, it was out of our hands. We were contracted to finish the job, so we had to stay until it was completed.

As the contract came to an end, we decided to present the *Bernadette* and its crew with a lifebelt, which had 'St Bernadette' printed on it. It was a sign of our appreciation for all their help. Little did we know there was a Judas on board.

Next day we were told some of the local lads were coming to O'Keefe's, a bar we used to drink at in the evening. Apparently they wanted a chat with us. 'That's nice of them,' I thought.

As we pulled up to the bar and ordered our Guinness, we could sense the atmosphere was a little tense. Most nights we'd have a good rapport with the bar staff and some of the locals, but this night was different.

In came the lads who were going to have a chat. The big one first, followed by a couple of others who stood by the door. 'Perhaps we should buy them a drink,' I thought. Show them how nice we are. Too late – Albert was at the big one like lightning. He gave him a 'Liverpool kiss'. If that's how they kiss in Liverpool, I thought, I'm staying in Norwich.

The guy went down as Albert pounded him with a couple of, what I thought were, low blows. Don't forget, at this time I was still something of a farm boy. Albert, on the other hand, had spent time in Wormwood Scrubs. It was only later I found out Albert had done the right thing as the big guy's intention was to do the same to us.

Suffice to say, I was learning – fast.

Next thing, the pub door flew open and the guys near the door got hold of their mate and started dragging him out. Albert gave the lad a big kick on his exit for his troubles. I peeked out of the door only to see them bundling him into the back seat of a car, and with a screech of tyres, they'd shot off up the road.

The whole thing only lasted a couple of minutes and I needed a drink. Thankfully I was in the right place.

Poor old Albert had hurt his hands. He had some sovereign rings on his fingers which had cut into his hands when he battered the lad. After a couple more pints we left and went back to our hotel.

The owner of the bar told us we might be in for another visit, as apparently the lads were from the local Sinn Féin. They wouldn't take kindly to what had just happened in the bar.

Next morning, there was a loud banging on our door. I opened it to find several policemen standing there. I don't remember asking them in, but in they came. The one with the most stripes told us to look out of the window where we'd see a car with a man reading a newspaper. Sure enough, when I looked, there was a man sat in a car pretending to read a newspaper.

I knew he was only pretending to read as when he saw me look, he raised it up as though he was reading it. It looked like a scene straight out of a Mickey Spillane movie – a bad one at that. Except this was no movie.

The boss policeman told us they'd had word there was a busload from the IRA heading our way to repay the previous evening's goings-on. It seemed they were keen to talk with a guy wearing several sovereign rings. It was then I noticed Albert had kept his hands under the bed covers.

The policeman said we had 15 minutes to get dressed and packed. They'd take us straight to Cork airport and put us on the first plane back to England, free of charge. As we left them at the aeroplane steps, they said goodbye and warned us not to come back for our own safety. They didn't need to repeat themselves.

Our visit to Ireland could have finished with a very sad ending.

Leaving countries in a hurry would become another common theme for me over the years. Cue Nigeria.

6

Not A Nice Place

I WAS quite excited when I landed my first job as an overseas air diver in the late 1960s. I had no idea it would be in Nigeria, but in all honesty, couldn't care less as I was in my 20s and getting a stamp to show off in my passport. However, it would soon become pretty clear as to why it was so easy to get a job here, especially as I wasn't very experienced at this time. The fact that Nigerians were still eating each other was not a great omen for my time ahead.

I left Heathrow on a British Caledonian flight with one stop in a place called Kano in northern Nigeria. It was just on the edge of the desert. We were scheduled to be there for an hour, so the pilot said, 'Please feel free to stretch your legs.'

We were parked just off the runway. No air conditioning or tunnels to the terminal, just a stewardess pointing to the stairs telling us to go down. The minute I stepped outside, the heat was horrible but not quite as horrible as the local at the bottom of the steps with a gun, who was staring me dead in the eyes.

I had never seen anyone that close with a gun before – especially one that was pointing at me. I almost missed the last step trying not to look at him or the barrel.

Undeterred, I followed the other passengers to the ruins they called the airport terminal. There was a distinct indescribable pungent smell and a storm of flies of all sizes and varieties landing on me, accompanied by the sound of one fan slowly rotating, looking and sounding like it was desperate for oil. Being somewhat dehydrated, I seem to remember that I was quite looking forward to a nice cold beer and to relax in the lounge. Forget it – welcome to Nigeria.

Back on the plane, I had a new companion in the seat beside me. It was a large smelly woman who not only filled her chair up but spilled over into mine, and who was sweating like a fountain. To top it off her perfume smelt like a cross between camel shit and cat poo with the stronger scent being cat poo. The good news was, we only had a couple of hours left to go.

She tried to talk to me, bless her, but her smell was just that little bit too overpowering, so I thought 'act dead' as I pretended to sleep. All I remember thinking was, 'I wish I had brought a clean pair of underpants and a shirt, as it's really hot in here.'

In Lagos she turned and gave me a wink and then disappeared with all the other locals, leaving me in a big queue which was specially for non-Nigerian nationals. I think I was almost as nervous with that wink as I was with the guy with the gun.

I had been told that our agent would be meeting me just as soon as we had cleared customs, but I wasn't expecting my name to be called out before I had got to the immigration desk.

I acknowledged this short, fat guy with a pair of sunglasses doing the calling, who had a sweat patch that looked like the map of Africa on the front and back of his light blue shirt. He came over smiling and asked for my passport. I thought, 'Hmmm – don't feel comfortable parting with my passport,' but as I said, I was new at this and decided to have faith in him. Thankfully, he was my chaperone, looking out for my best interests and didn't leave my side, right the way up to the passport desk.

It wasn't until he handed me back the passport and then in turn I handed it to the immigration guy behind the desk that I realised my man had put a couple of fairly big Nigerian bank notes inside it.

When I got the passport back the money had gone and was replaced with a big stamp. I didn't have any trouble clearing customs.

The agent later told me that's how things worked in Lagos. He said, 'It's the same when you leave – money changes hands or you don't leave.' That was to be the first of many lessons learnt about what would turn out to be the land of no rules and enmity.

Later I would find out that leaving also came with its own mini dramas. You paid your airport tax in US dollars, got your change in Nigerian currency, which they then immediately confiscated because you were not allowed to take their currency out of the country. I used to say, 'Hang on, I am not going to take it out, I am going to give it to the boot boy in the departure lounge.' That did the trick.

It was the same on the plane: you paid in British pounds or US dollars and got change in Nigerian naira. You soon learned to only carry small denominations.

My first visit was a couple of months before the end of the Nigerian civil war and there were lots of armed soldiers about. I later found out that most of them never had any bullets – they used to get pissed and fire them up in the air.

With all the hostility on land, I was really looking forward to getting into the water.

The sea of Nigeria was pretty clear and when the sun beat down it was like swimming in a gigantic fish tank. Most of the jobs would be around an existing platform of some kind, so the fish in their incredible colours and shapes would always congregate around it, pecking away at the legs.

As opposed to the North Sea where all marine life I'd ever seen were shades of brown and grey, in the form of cod, saithe and ling, this was quite eye-catching stuff. Perhaps a little too eye-catching though.

Every time you looked behind, there was a barracuda looking you straight in the eyes. At about six feet long, they looked quite scary with their double hinged jaws and big white teeth.

We always had a spear gun with us, not as you might think for protection, but for shooting the fish. The camp boss on the beach would pay us half a crown for a pound of fresh fish. We had a big compressed air gun with a three-foot spear, which I used to buy off the shelf from Lillywhites in London. Don't think you'd be able to do that these days.

These guns were very expensive and we had to buy a couple of extra spears with a boxful of barbs for the end. As they didn't sell things like that in Nigeria, we would stock up before we left the UK.

As time went on we discovered the best way to set the gun up. We used to fix a thin helicopter wire from the spear to the gun and a quarter-inch poly prop rope from the gun to the ocean surface, where one of the helpers would be on the end of the rope.

Once we had jumped into the water and selected a fish to shoot, we would fire, give the line a quick tug, and one of the helpers named Friday (actually his name) would pull it up, take it off the spear, reload the gun and send it back down.

Red snappers were everywhere, weighing in at as much as 25lb. It was not unusual to shoot 15–20 at a time. Although I wasn't out there to be a fisherman, the extra cash didn't hurt!

We weren't limited to just red snappers. Barracuda, groupers, lemon fish, yellow tail – the sea was awash with a multitude of magnificent fish. We always used to give Friday and his mate one.

Another kind of fishing we engaged in, was when the rig abandoned a well. On our 70-foot long boat with a crew of about eight people, we'd have to take the explosive man with his sackful of dynamite to blow the old well away.

The guy was a local. God knows who'd trained him. He used to appear with this big sack of explosives and a box of detonators with some wire. The explosives were red tubes which he would tape together, then stick a bunch of detonators in and ask us to take them down to the caisson that was going to be blown up.

We'd feed them down the inside of the pipe, about three feet below the surface, with a weight attached so they stayed down, then we'd come back up with the wire and give it to him on the deck. We never let him connect the wire to the box until we were well away.

When we reached the end of the wire he would connect it to the magic box, wind the handle round and round a few times, press the button, then put his fingers in his ears.

First time it felt like I was on the set of *The Bridge on the River Kwai*. The water plumed up in the air, the deck rattled, and my legs shook. I thought we were going to sink.

Once we got our breath back and things stopped vibrating, the old guy would go wild with excitement, jumping up and down pointing to all the fish that kept popping up. The explosion had killed them, blowing their lungs clean out of their mouths. Not very sporting, but effective. A bit of a perk for the old boy.

The captain asked for longer wire next time.

Below the surface, you would have about 70 feet of clear water, but once you got 30 feet from the bottom you would go into complete blackness and I mean black – you couldn't even see the glass in your mask.

Those waters came with a whole host of new creatures, most of which you could never see clearly. I've bumped into my fair share of sea snakes, most of which would have been deadly, but on the whole were very placid creatures. My concern was always, 'What do I do if I get bitten?' I'd have never be able to describe the slippery bugger to the medic – if I'd got that far.

Sharks were also in abundance in these waters, but they used to stay away from us divers. To my knowledge, in the history of commercial diving, I can't think of any shark attacks which resulted in fatalities.

We both swum at depth and kept ourselves to ourselves. They seemed to be more interested in what was swimming on the surface. As opposed to scuba divers who were swimming around and flapping, we would be walking around the ocean floor, getting on with our jobs.

Back to the murky depths, people would often ask me, 'Couldn't you use a torch?' Yes, you could have a torch in those waters, but if you've ever driven a car in fog – thick, pea-souper fog – and switched your lights on, you know it doesn't help much. And under there a torch didn't help at all.

Nigeria is one of the biggest deltas in the world and all the mud flows into the sea which is what makes it so black.

This particular day it was a pretty routine dive. Go down to the manifold and open a subsea valve at the end of a subsea loading hose. The other end was connected to an oil tanker ready to be loaded.

Down I went into the mud, following the line from the surface to find the first valve and open it, counting the turns. For some reason you had to report how many turns it took to open the valve. From memory it was 24 and as long as you reported the number of turns allocated to open that valve, everyone was happy.

Crossing over to the second valve I swam into a grouper. It was rumoured that Charlie, the 800lb grouper, lived down here. He'd been spotted once or twice, but not by me. He'd even been shot at a couple of times, but each time the spear had been lost. Legend had it the spears bounced off him.

It was at this point I realised Charlie was no myth. There was a thrash of a large tail fin, as I'd just disturbed him, and he took off with a big whoosh. It frightened the absolute shit out of me and took me a couple of minutes to compose myself. When my heart rate was back to normal I discovered I'd somehow got underneath the grating that the manifold was sitting on. All I could feel was the grating above me. This time following the bubbles was not an option. I moved about in the mud trying to find how I had managed to get under the grating but all I could feel was grating and more grating.

Remember, panic kills.

When things like this happen your breathing rate doubles because you get scared. It's a mistake because the tank on your back only has a certain amount of air in it and once that's gone, so are you.

On the bit you stick in your mouth – called a 'demand valve' which is what delivers gas to the diver while they're breathing in – you have what they call a 'contents gauge'; this tells you how much air you have left in the scuba tank. Lot of good it was going to do me down there in the murky black, unless it was written in braille.

The gauge normally floats behind you just out of reach. I think they've tightened up on that now and you stick it under your harness somehow.

Every breath seemed like the last one and my mind started going funny. They say it takes eight minutes to drown, in four of which you are still conscious. I remember thinking, 'Thank goodness I left my watch on the surface.'

The chances of them finding me under the grating would be slim, and if they did, there might not have been much left of me between the giant fish, sharks and snakes waiting for dinner.

All the time I was frantically trying to find a way out. The ingredients for an utter nightmare started to come together quickly. Mud, darkness, grating, a very limited supply of oxygen in the tank, carnivorous creatures and the sound of my heart beating. I've heard stories of divers who had been trapped and been found with half their fingers scratched away where they have been clawing to get out. There's no great way to die, but that's pretty bad. I remember thinking about my mum – she always said something like this would happen if I kept doing this job. Thanks mum.

In the Hollywood movies the hero pushes the grating up and it pops out. That was not the case today. Things were looking pretty grim and it got even worse when things I was touching started to squiggle out of my hands. My mind started to go doolally.

I was trying to tell myself not to panic, but as much as I tried, something had to give. It's a good job I didn't have any comms to the surface or they might have heard a grown man scream… and scream.

I decided to say a prayer – if I knew one. Then I remembered the one we used to say at school, 'Our Father…errr…please get me out from under this fucking grating.' I'm not sure if it went exactly like that when I was at school, but on that day, that was the version I went with.

Then, suddenly, my hand went up and touched…nothing. I can tell you, there's no better feeling than feeling no grating, despite being in pitch black.

Out I went. It took me a few moments to take stock and get my shit together but I remembered I had another 24 turns before I could follow the bubbles to the surface.

On the way up, with the bubbles, I remember thinking, 'Fuck you, Charlie!' Friday was smiling when I got back on to the deck. It was good to see a friendly face again.

Sitting on the deck of the crew boat in the sun on the way back to the oil camp I was thinking, 'I am going to murder a few ice cold beers tonight.'

7

Escravos

THE camp I was stationed at had just been attacked by the famous Red Barron: a Swedish mercenary pilot. He had shot up some of the oil storage tanks. The anti-aircraft gun at the end of the pier had missed him completely. The sign at the camp gate said, 'Welcome to Escravos – remember to keep your head down'.

About 100 people lived on this remote oil camp, which was called Escravos – the Portuguese word for slave. It gained its name as a result of the location being a prominent slave trading area between the USA and Nigeria in the 18th century.

The camp was run by Gulf Oil and you could only get there by air or sea. When we arrived, it was shifts of three months on and a month off. Not a bad life for a young diver.

Three months of captivity then a month of mayhem. I used to live in Menorca for a month in those days as a tax exile. I say tax exile but they got it all back eventually.

At Escravos they had three offshore tanker loading buoys a couple of miles out to sea. These buoys were connected to the subsea manifold by big rubber hoses with a 24-inch diameter. Going up and down all day, every day meant they needed changing every year.

When this happened we'd bring in another six divers from the UK to help. It wasn't a tricky job, just labour-intensive and pretty dirty.

In those days they never had any means of flushing the oil out of the pipes. We would go down and close the subsea valves, 24 turns on both, then go underneath the buoy with a big hammer and spanner, put the spanner on the nut and smash merry hell out of it with the big hammer until they were all loose. At this point the oil would start gushing out into the sea.

It went everywhere. Thick crude oil would cover your whole body, cover your mask, get in your hair. You name it, it got in there, including up your bum. Saying that, it did make swimming easier – no squeaking. We'd beat a hasty retreat until all the oil was out of the pipe and all that was left was a mile-long oil slick drifting out to sea.

Nowadays, if you spill so much as a pint of oil there's a full-scale inquiry – and so there should be. Not just because of the harm it does to the marine life, but because at the time of writing this book, the stuff costs $120 a barrel.

After work we used to ring through to the room boy, Joseph, and order a couple of ice cold Star beers and some warm Go Go's. God knows why they called them Go Go's as they were really just peanuts – slightly warm with plenty of salt. Either way, I loved them with a bottle of Star beer. The beer had more impurity in it than a septic tank but once you could hold a couple of bottles down without having to go to the toilet, it tasted fine.

There were all sorts of nationalities in the camp, but it was the Italian boat captains I remembered fondly. These guys were the pilots for bringing the tankers into the loading buoys, and they were also a good source of whiskey and cigarettes.

The pilots had the customs guys in their pockets and smoothed things along. That's how things worked in Nigeria back then. For a small profit they would sell the whiskey and cigarettes on to us.

The Italians would keep in with us divers, as it wasn't unheard of for them to run over a mooring rope or two with their tankers, which would consequently get jammed in their tanker's propeller. On a number of occasions I would be one of the divers jumping in to untangle it.

There would always be a load of shouting and arm waving when this happened, but nobody ever got blamed as it was of course never their fault.

Those mooring ropes used to cost an arm and a leg and by the time we had finished hacking them out of the propellers they were worthless. The locals used to love these jobs as we would give the old rope to them and they would use it for making fishing nets. Although, they had to be careful as to where and how they would spread their nets out on the beach.

On the tide line you could see old coconut tree roots, where the tree had gone leaving a short stump with a hole in the middle. The locals used to take a dump in the centre of the stump at low tide, wait until after high tide then it was empty just like a modern toilet – only difference was it took six hours to flush.

We used to party quite a lot at night and this was where the whiskey used to come in handy.

One night we were in George the welder's room. George was one of many Lebanese people on site and was a good source of gold.

That particular night I bought an eight-piece puzzle ring made from 18-carat gold – it was good stuff. He was showing me how to take it apart and put it back together again, trouble was, the more whiskey I had the more complicated it became and in the end nobody could do it, not even George the welder. Good excuse for another party.

The cosmopolitan mix on site made the camp very entertaining.

There was a bunch of helicopter pilots, many of whom had served in Vietnam. Good guys but a bit unstable, most likely as a result of the war having had a bad effect on them. One of them flew his helicopter inside an empty oil tank on site. Once inside he found that he couldn't get enough lift to get himself out again and had to keep going round and round until he finally managed to get out. I don't think that he did it again after that time.

Another one of them had only been there two days when he was doing a routine collection at one of the offshore platforms. He'd landed and was waiting for the man with the fire extinguisher to come and open the door but there was no one. Being an ex-Vietnam vet and having no fear, he decided to go and find someone. He jumped out of his helicopter, leaving it ticking over ready for a quick exit, and went down to the helilounge, only to find they were just finishing their fish stew. Everything stopped for fish stew. You couldn't blame them – it was damn good stuff.

Well, he gave them all a bollocking for keeping him waiting and marched back up to the helideck.

As he got to the deck, he shouted out 'GOD DAMMIT!!!!' as his helicopter had blown over the side into the sea and was slowly sinking below the waves. He left the next day.

We recovered the helicopter a few days later, but its best flying days were now behind it.

There's a bit of a theme of helicopters and helidecks during my diving days and unfortunately, none of them end up with fairytale endings. The next episode was no exception.

8

George The Welder

W E got a call one morning from the camp superintendent, an American guy called Dale. He shouted out, 'GET YOUR ASSES DOWN TO THE CREW BOAT AS FAST AS YOU CAN.' There'd been a big explosion on the berth loading platform and one of the helicopters had reported that the helideck had been blown clean off the top.

The platform is the point that the pipeline from the beach comes to before going to the loading buoys which are further out. It's where the Italian captains stayed when they were waiting for a tanker to come in ready for mooring up.

Everyone was looking for the boss, captain Luigi, as they were trying to find out if any of his people were on the platform when the explosion happened. Their cabin was right under the helideck.

There was a firefighting vessel on its way with a crew who went to the platform to sort things out, make things safe, and see if they could find anyone. They normally had a list of who was on board at any one time but nobody could find it. At this point it was more concern than panic.

The boat trip was about an hour from where we were, so we got our equipment sorted out and had a chat with the captain, who was from the deep south of the US, Louisiana. Nice guy, who I'd met a number of times before and who always asked me to read the letters he'd received from his wife. I'm not sure how much schooling he'd had in Louisiana, but boy could he drive a boat. He'd learned when he was at home in the swamps, and Nigeria must have been very similar territory for him to tackle. In addition to reading the letters from his wife, he also used to ask me to write them on his behalf, which must have amused his wife as a result of my dyslexia. I also always used to put a little bit extra in, to make for fun reading. She couldn't wait for him to get home.

Back on the vessel, the radio on the bridge blared out so loud, you could almost hear it back on the beach.

It appeared all the Italians had been accounted for. The only person we couldn't find was George the welder, who had been doing a repair job on the surge tank at the time of the explosion. The surge tank is what it says – it takes any excess oil in the system. The fire and rescue team unfortunately couldn't find any trace of George or his helper. They'd located his welding torch and rods but that was it.

When we got there, the platform looked a bit strange without the helideck, which had now sunk to the bottom of the ocean. The platform was still smoking a bit but, apart from that, it looked pretty normal.

I dived off the crew boat to see if I could locate the helideck and put a buoy on it so it was ready for recovery.

One of the fire guys came aboard soon after to have a chat and told me what they thought had happened.

It appeared at first glance that George had struck an arc under the surge tank with his burning torch, which consequently blew the tank. Either no one had told him or he hadn't understood the tank still had oil in it. This sort of thing happened when many different nationalities were involved – simple breakdown of communication, but that deadly nod of the head acknowledging 'yes', when you are 'not sure', can have its consequences down the line.

I jumped over the side and went down the nearest leg. Seemed like a good place to start the search. There were lots of fish in the water that day, and as terrible as it sounds, if there were any human parts floating around, they would be a great guide as they would have flocked to the food and started nibbling.

The helideck must have woken them up as it passed on its way to the bottom. I thought to myself, 'I'll never find it if it's in the mud.' I hated doing circular searches on the bottom in the mud. But they wanted their helideck back and there was no option.

Those circular searches nearly ended in disaster for me on a number of occasions. The way these searches work are quite simple.

You have a down line with a weight on the end and you lower the weight down until it hits the bottom. You then swim down the line until you get to the weight. Next you undo the rope that you have tied to the weight, which would be a certain length – i.e. 30 feet, 40 feet etc. This length would be stretched out tight in order to be able to swim or walk round in a circle. As you started to walk, you would either bump into something or the rope would snag on something. In black water you have to guess as best you can when you have done a circle, and hope what had just snagged the rope does not have a big set of teeth.

On one occasion we were sent out to look for a supply boat's anchor that had got lost. The captain had taken a reference of the area so he knew where it was.

'Over there,' they said, pointing. I thought, 'It's a big ocean. I could do with a little more direction here.' It was shallow so I jumped off the port side and stayed out in 'that direction'. There was a lazy swell running but I should have been okay once I was on the bottom which was about only about 30 feet down.

The bottom, surprise surprise, was pitch black and I really had no idea where I was. I had an iron bar which I would hammer into the sea bed and 20 feet of rope. Once the iron bar was in, I uncoiled the rope to full length and, keeping it tight, I started going round in a circle hoping I could entangle the anchor at some point – that's if I was going to be lucky enough to find it.

The best place for your mind when doing this is in neutral.

Well, I was in neutral when I felt my back being pressed down by something and the pressure kept getting worse. I figured I'd somehow managed to get underneath the boat and it was pushing me into the mud. Not good. I was beginning to think it was going to crush me or break my back, when it started, ever so slowly, to lift. It must have been going up on the swell. As I knew this was my chance to get out, I took it. Once it was off me, I gave four quick pulls on the swim line which told the surface that I wanted my swim line slack to be pulled up, followed by me.

It turned out that what little tide there was had swung the boat around and it ended up over the top of me. I remember thinking, 'Fuck the anchor – let's have one of those cold beers.'

Back to George the welder.

I was just above the mud line looking around, when I saw a grey mass in the distance which could have been the helideck. I thought, 'That would be a bit of luck if it is – it will save me swimming around in the mud.' I made my way over to it and, sure enough, it was the deck. It must have been a big bang as the deck had cleared everything and landed the right way up, 20-odd feet from the base of the platform. I thought I'd have a look about so I could give a comprehensive report when I came up.

The safety netting round the outside was even intact. All in all it looked in pretty good shape. I saw a big grouper sitting on one side of the deck, looking at me. It was seriously ugly, big and I had no idea whether it was looking at me out of pure interest or as its next meal option. I was a diver, not an expert in marine life, and wasn't keen to find out first hand its eating preferences. I did have a quick moment to wonder if it might have been Charlie's brother or girlfriend.

There was a shackle laying on the helideck, so I banged it in front of the grouper to scare him. He looked at me and I thought, 'Oh shit!' So I got a bit closer and did it again. This time it worked and it moved about five feet away. I did it a few more times – bang, back five, bang, back five. We'd done about 15 feet when I spotted what looked like George's welding hat. Welders always wear these colourful little hats to stop the sparks burning their heads. 'Brilliant,' I thought. 'At least I can take his hat back.' It was only on closer inspection I realised he was still wearing it.

I felt a bit sick. Not that I was going to throw up, but a feeling came over me that reminded me I was human. This was the first time I'd seen human remains floating in the ocean – but unfortunately would not be the last by a long stretch.

The situation was desensitised by the fact that I was wearing gloves, a diving suit and had a helmet on, which meant I couldn't smell or feel anything. With him also having a welder's hat on, I couldn't feel the fibres of his hair or texture of his skin, but seeing the sinew and stuff hanging out from his neck was a reminder of how shocking a situation this was. I had to keep reminding myself, 'You've got a job to do here Beckett. Turn off all emotions and bring the hat back on board.' I'd learn over time that witnessing the moment a person became injured or died was far worse than seeing them dead.

George's hat, with his head inside, had stuck in the underside of the net. There was no other part of him, just his head. His eyes were unfortunately missing. It didn't take long for the creatures below to get to work on him. That grouper must have also been trying to get him but hadn't thought about going underneath the wire. Well, being a diver, I soon worked it out.

We never did find his body, so I decided to get George's head so he could be sent home for a decent burial, but the only thing I could find to put him in was an empty five-gallon can. I didn't fancy carrying his head with all those fish about, so into the tin his head went and up to the surface we came. I don't think Friday and his mate were expecting to see what was in the can.

My mate Allan, the other diver, took over. I knew he could handle things like this as he used to be a military policeman in Aden, Yemen, and unfortunately, part of his culture at that time involved bombs and dead bodies.

Allan was a good guy. I remember when he cut his leg quite badly on some razor-like barnacles and needed to go to hospital for treatment. There was a local in the bed next to him. Allan asked what was up with him. The guy said he'd cut three of his fingers off. Quick as a flash, kind old Allan says, 'Never mind, they'll grow again.' It brought a big smile from the guy. I'm not sure they ever did grow back though.

That night it was a bit sad. No George at the party. Things worked out with the puzzle rings, as we got another Lebanese welder.

We wouldn't let him wear George's hat, though. There was only one George and he was sorely missed.

9

Certainly Not Football

BEFORE my rapid departure from Nigeria in 1972, we'd been sent down to Port Harcourt to do a diving job with some other guys from a different company.

We were staying at the Port Harcourt Country Club. It was a leftover from the colonial days and you could see it used to be nice, but at that time, I steered clear of drinking the water coming out of its taps, on the grounds that it was brown. The only semi-confidence I had in any drinking fluid at that point in Nigeria was Star beer and a few other select alcoholic beverages.

The en suite smelled of drains, there were brown stains in the loo, and lots of those little transparent things that crawled up the wall, but it was okay. The swimming pool area was quite nice, once you'd checked for deadly snakes such as cobras and puff adders.

It was only Saturday and we didn't have to go to work until Monday so we thought we'd lie around the pool, smoke some dope, have a few gin and tonics, top up the tan, and generally chill out. When it was not the rainy season, the weather could be quite nice, that's if you liked near-100 per cent humidity.

It was Allan who first suggested we try smoking some weed or grass a few weeks earlier. You could get it quite easily in Nigeria so we asked Friday to ask around for us.

Next day he'd located a source – turned out to be the chief immigration officer. Friday said we must give him 50 naira (equivalent to about 15 pence) and he'd get us some. I thought, 'You won't get much for 50 naira but it should be enough to get started.' We gave him the money and asked if the guy could come over the next night and show us how it worked. All I knew was you rolled it up like a cigarette, lit it, took a few puffs and waited. Friday said the guy would come to the room that night and show us how to do it.

It arrived in a carrier bag stuffed full of, what looked like, dead grass seeds. I'll never get through all that, I thought. That night we got the Star beer and Go Go's as normal and thought we'd try this stuff without waiting for the immigration officer.

We had one, then another. Nothing happened. I thought we've been sold a dud. Ripped off for 50 naira. Typical, should have known better.

Knock, knock. It's him. The immigration guy had come to show us what to do. We shook hands and all that stuff and he started to roll one. It was all going good up the point when he stuck this enormous pink tongue out to lick the paper. At this point, our previous attempts kicked in. I looked at Allan and we both started laughing. The poor guy must have thought we'd gone nuts. We couldn't stop laughing even once he'd left the room. It was good stuff.

We gave it up soon after Allan got lost one night. One of the drillers found him standing asleep in his wardrobe.

Back to this particular Saturday afternoon.

The divers from the other company started to arrive. The diving world was pretty small and you got to work with most of the guys over a period of time. These guys were from a company called Solar Shell – not as well-known as ours but it was all right. I once went for a job interview there soon after I started air diving and started to tell the tale to these guys.

The man doing the interviewing was called Bill something. He worked for the Rank organisation who owned Solar Shell at the time. We were having a nice chat and I thought things were going well when he started asking what else I could do. Was I a welder? Was I a carpenter? Was I a sparky?

'Hang on, Bill. I thought I was being interviewed for a diving job?'

He replied, 'Monkeys can go to the moon. Monkeys could be divers. Look, do you want the job?'

'No thanks,' I said. 'Better get yourself a monkey.' With that, I left.

It wasn't until years later, when I'd started to mature a bit, that I thought he did have a point. Diving is just the means of transport to the work site. It's all about what you can do when you get down there. Anyone can breathe gas underwater – that is, except the locals.

Every now and again, we'd be under pressure (no pun intended) to train some of the locals to become divers, with interviews being held in the decompression chamber.

Part of the interview entailed a quick blowdown to see how they handled a bit of gas pressure. By the time we got them down to ten feet, they'd be holding their heads and pulling at the door screaming to get out. I'd say to Allan we should have shown them how to equalise their ears first.

Word soon got about and, if I remember correctly, we only had three applications. After the first one I always made sure I sat at the opposite end to the door as I was nearly crushed in his panic to get out.

Back with the boys from Solar Shell – the next day most of us were nursing hangovers. We'd sat about drinking and smoking that laughing weed until fairly late the night before, reliving some good times we'd had on our last bit of leave. Just for the record – those good times did not include the local girls, as sexually transmitted infections were rife.

We were getting ready to go to another job later that day, when around midday, an old clunky army lorry pulled up. Some soldiers got out of the back with rifles. I felt my bowels loosen. You did hear some worrying stories about those guys especially the ones with guns. I was wondering what they were doing, when one of them asked us to get into the back of the lorry. As one, we all said, 'On your bike.' When they raised their guns even the bravest diver fell silent. There's an old joke that goes, 'What do you call a local with a gun?' 'Sir' is the right answer.

The guy, to his credit, said he had his orders to take us to the football stadium to watch something. We all assumed it was to watch a football match. Not a bad deal really. I thought, 'This is nice. I'd have to pay 20 quid back home.' He said he'd bring us back to the club afterwards. As they had the guns we got in the back of the lorry and off we went.

The journey lasted about five minutes, and me and the other five guys started bullshit conversation to make out we were calm. The reality was we were crapping ourselves. You could tell we were all thinking the same things – do we jump off and leg it? Do we refuse to get off the truck? Do we try and overpower them? All the various options were halted by one sobering reality – these guys were all holding machine guns.

As there was a crowd of about 5,000 at the stadium, I figured it must be a big match. We were marched to the equivalent of the directors' box, but alas no Delia Smith. It all seemed a bit strange. They had a dozen posts in the centre circle and I wondered if there was going to be a firework display before the match. As I enjoyed a good firework display, I became a little more relaxed and settled down.

However – crowds watching firework displays tend to look excited, not nervous. Something was definitely not right. On looking around I noticed the crowds were all sitting on the same side of the stand which seemed rather unusual. Again, trying to use some kind of positive logic, I thought, 'Perhaps they would get the sun in their eyes if they sat over the other side?'

To add to the already bizarre set-up, a couple of cameramen came up and took several pictures of us. I assumed half a dozen white faces in the crowd must be unusual as we were pretty deep off the tourist track. When I asked one of them why he was taking photos, his reply turned out to be the beginning of an unpleasant afternoon. He said, 'There's going to be a display of local justice.' All my positive logic was starting to disappear from me. Mainly through my arse.

The crowd fell quiet as several armed soldiers came out and set up position with their backs to us, but facing the posts in the centre circle. It was right about now I got the gist of what was about to go down and also realised why we were all sitting on this side of the ground.

Once the soldiers were in position you could start to sense the unease in the crowd – it was palpable. Then, out came a dozen men wearing rags, with their hands tied behind their backs, escorted by a soldier who took each of them to a post and tied them to it. Those lads were screaming and shouting, many of them falling to the floor, begging for mercy, so it took a few minutes to get them tied up to their respective wooden posts. It was a barbaric scene that would make you cringe if it had been a movie, but to sit there and watch this in reality was one of the worst memories a man could take to the grave with him.

One by one they were blindfolded. Another soldier said something to each of them. We were too far away to hear what was said, but I don't think it was, 'What would you like for your last supper?'

Then it fell silent and the soldier in charge looked over to the men with the guns. When he raised his hand, the soldiers raised their guns and pointed them at the men tied to the poles. As his hand came down there was an almighty noise of semi-automatic guns which seemed to last forever. They were blowing arms and legs off all over the place. Then hush. Slowly the gun smoke dispersed and my head and ears stopped ringing. All you could hear was the sound of some of the guys in the middle still squealing. Hard to believe, but the soldiers had not managed to kill them all with the first volley.

The hand was raised again and lowered. Another deafening roar. Then, silence. The guy giving the orders then went round with a handgun and shot anyone in the head who showed any signs of life.

Then, as if nothing had happened, the soldiers that had taken us to the stadium took us back to the country club about 30 minutes later. On the ride back, I said to the others guys, 'Did we actually just witness a public execution?' They all nervously mumbled, 'I think so.' The soldiers didn't say a word. Very uncomfortable.

Talk about fuck up a Sunday. Try drinking a gin and tonic with your ears still ringing.

We had our photos in the paper the next day, with the caption of 'White Men See Justice'. We never did find out what crimes they had committed but apparently they were petty. I'd hate to have seen how they dealt with major crimes. Not sure about justice, but I certainly saw the scene at that stadium in my head many times over in the years to come.

My drama was unfortunately not over yet. On the way home a couple of weeks later, I was coming out of the hotel near the airport in Lagos, when suddenly it all went black. When I woke up, I realised I'd been robbed. I'd been hit on the head from behind and they took everything – my money, watch, shoes, bag. I remember thinking they should have taken my socks. I had a $100 bill folded up inside and my passport in my back pocket. I did look a bit funny when I rocked up to the airport with no shoes, but the bill helped me through.

I began to think I'd been in Nigeria too long but I kept giving the country the benefit of the doubt that I'd just been unlucky with my experiences to date. However, the next mini-episode was almost the straw breaking the camel's back.

One day, I was sitting on the back of a tugboat ready to do a dive. We were looking for a damaged pipeline as one of the supply boats had dragged its anchor across it. Not an uncommon event. I mentioned before those guys from Louisiana could drive the boats well but their reading of nautical charts was a bit iffy.

There I was, fully kitted out. We'd got a bit more modern by this time – we had lightweight helmets which had a hose pipe to the surface and, would you believe, gave us communications with the surface. Not to mention, they also kept your head dry. It took a bit of getting used to as once it was on and you were underwater, if you got an itch on your face you couldn't get to it. You tried moving your face in every direction but you never seemed to be able to scratch it. Most annoying.

The other problem was they had a harness that went from the helmet through your crotch and back to the helmet which, when pulled tight, could be pretty uncomfortable. You had to be prepared. I'm sure Friday used to pull it too tight on purpose. I threatened to cut his fish rations on many occasions.

Friday wasn't with me this particular day. We had a new guy who was sitting across the deck from me. The boat was rolling about, as boats do, when this guy started to retch. Poor sod, I thought, he's going to be sick. It's not nice being seasick. Many people struggle with it, even hardened sailors. Anyway, you'd normally be sick over the side as it saved cleaning up. But not this guy. He did it right between his legs. Great, I thought. Just what I needed before this guy was about to place my diving helmet on.

I looked away as you do, out of respect, but when I looked back he was going through it and picking bits out. I shouted at him to stop and wash it away, but he looked at me as though I'd ruined his lunch. I remember thinking, 'That's not normal.' It was bloody horrible.

For the rest of that dive I imagined him going through it and eating the big bits.

Believe it or not, the public execution, my mugging, Charlie the grouper or even the diver eating his own puke, were not my reasons for leaving Nigeria. A short while after I was mugged, I was walking through the camp when someone stood in front of me and refused to move. I was tired and short-tempered and unloaded a rather unpleasant tirade of words his way, only to find out he was a well-respected Nigerian oil person.

In turn, he reported me to the camp superintendent, who then knocked on my door later that evening. 'We need to get you out of here quick David. You've upset the wrong person and if you hang around, you may well be "hung around".'

Before I knew it, I was on the next Cessna light aircraft from Escravos to Lagos, followed by the first plane out of Lagos, which was an Alitalia flight to Rome, swiftly followed by a flight back to the UK.

Thank you Nigeria and goodbye – forever.

10

Milk Bottles

SOON after exiting Nigeria, I headed for the North Sea, which apart from having a different climate and culture, also had a number of episodes lined up for my future timeline that would test me to the limit. Due to my age and erratic living habits, I didn't think about buying a place to settle.

Instead, in between contracts in the early 1970s, I lived with a mate of mine called Ron, who used to sell second-hand cars from his house in a bit of an Arthur Daley-type set-up. Anyway, he decided he was going to get married, but before he did, we were going to have one last blowout in Marbella.

Unfortunately he'd got himself so excited about the holiday that he became constipated. At Heathrow I told him to go and get some Ex-Lax from the chemist which he did. Having experienced constipation as a diver, I knew just how potent this stuff was. It's a bit of a wolf in sheep's clothing as it comes in the form of what looks like a chocolate bar. Two tiny little squares from this bad boy is enough to unclog the most stubborn of colons.

When he came back I asked if he had got some and he replied, 'Yes. It said on the wrapper eat like chocolate so I ate the whole bar.' Although I had an idea of how the next few hours might pan out, I knew there would be no merit to being the fortune teller on this occasion as we boarded the plane. The damage had been done.

After about five minutes of sitting down, his stomach made a deep slurring noise, followed by what sounded like a plunger dislodging a giant bubble. We both looked down at his stomach and laughed. He still hadn't clocked on.

The trolley dolly was asking us what we would like to drink when the Ex-Lax really kicked in and he had to make a dash for the toilet without being able to answer her. He didn't move from the loo until the call for landing was announced.

After checking in to the Don Pepe hotel in Marbella, he was so ill I had to get the local doctor to bung him up with some stuff. It took Ron a while to get his confidence back. He had got some Fred Trueman-type white trousers especially for his holiday, but he didn't dare wear them until the last couple of days.

On the way home he asked what I was going to do as I would have to leave the house when he got married. He went on to suggest that I tried to settle down a bit and that I put a bit of time into looking for a steady girlfriend. He hinted about a girl who I'd met at the local pub a few weeks prior.

I never did much about it until one night I was at a 21st birthday party and saw her again with another guy. It struck me then just how beautiful she was. I asked her to dance and to the annoyance of the other fella, stole her from right underneath him. Three months later, in 1973, we got married. Forty-three years later we are still together.

Quite often, in those days, it made the headlines in the papers if a North Sea diver died or if North Sea divers got stuck in a diving bell and required rescuing.

It would have frightened a lot of the divers' wives but not mine – she was tough. Although, she always carried the life insurance policy in her handbag. Come to think of it, she has lots of handbags – belts, shoes, and clothes too, but that's another story.

The diving she could cope with, but me coming back after a few pints with my mates was another story. The dents on the boot of my Triumph Stag paid tribute to the nights I was late, as she would hurl milk bottles at it. It did her head in when they changed to plastic bottles.

On my return from Nigeria, and now a newlywed, I started working on a derrick barge in the Ekofisk oil field (in the Norwegian sector of the North Sea) doing surface gas diving.

Surface gas diving is when you go down in a basket lowered from the surface. You start off breathing air and, when you reach a depth of around 40 feet, you switch from breathing air to gas. We called it gas but it was actually a heliox mix (more helium than oxygen). The helium made your voice sound all squeaky, like Donald Duck, and the oxygen kept you alive. This type of diving has been banned now in the UK, along with bounce diving, on the grounds of safety and how hard it was on the diver's body.

The radio on the surface from which the dive supervisor talked to you, had a helium unscramble, which was supposed to change your voice back to normal, though most of them never used it. Seems they preferred talking to Donald Duck sound-alikes, which says a lot about divers.

When you changed from air to gas it got much colder and seemed to be cleaner. Your head stayed clear the further you went down. If you stayed breathing air, as you got deeper you'd become disorientated and would probably pass out. This is what they call 'the Martini effect' – the phrase was coined as you think you're invincible. You could be 200 feet below the surface and think it's a good idea to walk on the ocean floor without your mask on. Bit like being drunk, but in a far deadlier environment. So you breathe this gas mix to help keep you sane(ish).

When you've finished what you're doing and start coming up, you have to switch back to air. At around 100 feet you can hear the air coming down the umbilical and all of a sudden it's in your helmet. It's hard to explain unless you've experienced it, but when the air arrives, it's like inhaling a muddy dark mixture, which in turn has you hanging on to the basket in case you pass out. The feeling soon passes and you feel okay again.

We used to switch back to air as soon as we could as there was more oxygen in air than in the gas mix which helped with the decompression. They'd actually banned this type of diving already at that time, but the company we were working for had received special dispensation to continue. A lot of this went on in the early days – anything you couldn't do legally you got special dispensation for. Quite handy, really.

I say I never panicked, because panic kills, but the closest I ever did was around this time. Back then, they used to mix the gas in dive control on the boat and pump it down to you through a thing called a mix-maker. If you wanted 11 per cent oxygen and the rest helium, then that's what the guy in dive control would give you through your umbilical. However, the systems to check if anything was wrong were not great. There was no guarantee that the oxygen part had been mixed in or if it was twice the dose. I remember looking at the mixer once before I was supposed to be diving and the mix of oxygen was way low and it turned out he had just forgotten about it. I guess lightning struck twice.

On this particular occasion I started to feel a bit funny, swiftly followed by apprehensive as my breathing became difficult. When you have bad gas pumped down through your tube, there's only one place it's going and that's through the diver's lungs. I was making my way back to the bell and was just about to pop my head up to take my helmet off to breathe some proper stuff, when the guy in dive control must have clocked on and the slug of bad stuff passed. Thankfully they did away with the mix-makers after a few years and had the stuff pre-mixed on shore, which was mixed, tested and then given to the divers. I guess I was part of a learning curve for the commercial diving industry at that point.

As you neared the surface you'd have to stop at 40 feet and rest there for a certain time dependent on how long you had dived. The same again at 30 feet. These stops are called 'in-water decompression stops'. They were the start of the decompression process. At 30 feet you might even be given pure oxygen, although you had to be careful with that stuff as at over 60 feet it could become poisonous and burn your lungs.

Once you'd done your time at 30 feet, the basket would be lifted to the surface were there was a mad rush to get you undressed, throw you into a decompression chamber, and blow you down to 30 feet again breathing oxygen. This all had to be done in less than four minutes.

Once you were at 30 feet and in the chamber, you followed the decompression schedule until the oxygen washed the nitrogen bubbles out of your system. This method is not used anymore. In fact, you can now only dive to 50 metres (164 feet). The risk of getting the bends using surface gas jumping was fairly high, so the diving threshold makes sense.

Thankfully, my gas and bounce diving days were numbered.

11

Rolls-Royce Diver

O NE day, I was working on the sea bed when I bumped into another diver who was working off a dive boat stationed at the other side of the platform I was working from. I was gas diving at the time.

He was working for a company called Scan Dive, and as opposed to myself, who had a 320-foot umbilical dropping down from the surface, this guy had a 65-foot umbilical coming out of his diving bell. He was a saturation diver.

We had a thumbs-up session and a shout at each other. I never understood why we did that as you could never hear what they were shouting. It must have been murder for the dive supervisor sitting on the surface with his headset on, as it must have done his bloody eardrums in.

Saturation diving was considered to be a lot safer than surface gas diving and they got paid a great deal more. You would do one decompression at the end of 28 days as opposed to every day, which is what I was doing as a surface gas diver. There was far less stress on the body. I remember thinking, 'I must apply for a job with those guys' – and I did.

After I'd finished diving on that barge, I rang up Scan Dive and they asked me a few questions about my qualifications and diving experience, and asked me in for an interview.

In those days you could bullshit a bit and you didn't need any particular kind of certification. References? What references!

Divers needed to be multi-skilled and should have been able to burn a pipeline, operate a hydraulic frame etc. most of which I could do, but in the interview I told a wee white lie and said I'd done a fair bit of bell diving. To be fair, I had done some but not a great deal.

Still, I figured it couldn't be that difficult. Turns out I was right. I got the job and, with that, began saturation diving in 1973.

I was now a commercial saturation diver, which although had only been around a handful of years, was considered to be the Rolls-Royce of diving – as real divers do it deeper and longer.

Why is it called 'saturation' I hear you ask? Simply because the body's tissues become saturated in nitrogen while in the chamber.

We had what was called a 'dive system', also known as a 'dive chamber', which was incorporated into the bowels of the vessel. It could be anything from a 12- to 24-man system. The system consisted of three or four chambers, one of which was a wet chamber with a small tube (trunking) and a door that led to the diving bell. The chambers varied in size from two metres by four metres to as big as four metres by six metres. Either way, it was pretty confined.

The whole purpose of saturation diving is to give 24-hour coverage to the job, by keeping divers on the work site at all times, as opposed to air diving where you have a given time at a particular depth. For example, (referring to my bible back then of the *U.S. Navy Diving Manual March 1970 Edition!*) as an air diver, if you went down to 70 feet, you would have 52 minutes of 'bottom time'. This basically meant you could work for 52 minutes without needing to decompress. The rule was that you would take approximately three minutes to swim to the surface from this depth, roughly 25 feet per minute. If your bottom time was 180 minutes, you would need to either take about 50 minutes to surface, or spend about 40 minutes in a chamber at 40 feet below the surface, on oxygen. Either would successfully decompress the diver.

If you went down to 170 feet on air, your bottom time was only seven minutes and you would spend roughly that time swimming back up to the surface. Stay down there for 40 minutes and you would take about 75 minutes to reach the surface safely. The accuracy and reliability of your watch was of paramount importance, which is why, certainly back in those days, many divers would be wearing a Rolex. I think they also liked to be a bit flash.

Air diving was also limited in so much as, you couldn't go to extreme depths. I'd be going as low as 520 feet at times and that was simply impossible on air.

With bell diving, you blew yourself down to the depth, did as much time as you could and then came back up. With saturation diving, because you were already in tune with the outside nitrogen levels, you could stay for 12 hours or even up to 14 or 16 as I used to do. Although these days they tend to be down for about six to eight hours maximum.

On the bigger systems you had two bells. One bell down there working and the other on the top. When the bell below was nearly finished, the other one went down, so they were ready to jump straight in without any periods of inactivity occurring on the task in hand.

It also worked out cheaper to have divers all ready and decompressed, ready to jump in and out as opposed to having them diving one by one in small periods. This also worked out better during bad weather as you were not near the splash zone as such. Vessels are expensive and the North Sea could be nigh on inhospitable. You had to take advantage of the good weather when it happened and having this system in place allowed that to happen.

Here's how you get saturated.

In principle, 12 divers are blown down in the chamber. Once you are in, they blow you down about 30 feet on air and then check for leaks, just to make sure the chamber is holding the pressure comfortably. Then they pump heliox in, until they get to the equivalent pressure at which they'll be working. There is not

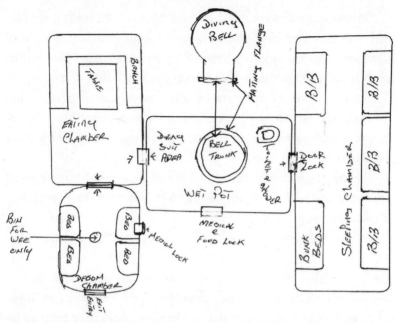

My hand drawing of where saturation divers live for a month.

a standard gas mix. Each job requires a different mix in relation to the depth. We would then stay at saturation while the divers exiting would start decompression, giving the uninterrupted 24/7 service to the task in hand.

Why do you need to decompress I hear you ask? Decompression is required to stop divers getting 'the bends' or bubbles in the blood which can be pretty nasty. Saturation diving was designed to reduce the risk of the bends, as opposed to the vulnerability with air, gas or scuba diving, due to the number of decompressions.

Now is probably a good time to explain further about the bends. Years before I'd got involved in this game, when divers used to surface after coming out of a compressed air environment, many displayed a number of issues, including the inability to be able to stretch their limbs, dizziness and in some cases, death. It took a number of years to establish why this was the case, and the guy credited with understanding why this happened on ascent was called Paul Bert. Certainly a pioneer.

If he hadn't worked out the need to come up slowly, many more lives would have been lost and diving would still be in the dark ages. The discovery would also be useful knowledge to anybody below sea level, not just those in water. As tunnels started to be built in abundance during the 1900s, many started to suffer. Stories of people celebrating in tunnels by opening bottles of champagne and being unimpressed with the bottle not popping, soon revisited that gas on their ascent.

Thankfully, with new knowledge in hand, 'tunnel decompression' for employees became the norm for those working below sea level.

I'm happy to say I never suffered from the bends. The closest I got was having a little niggle, which basically meant I felt something, but it didn't turn out to be a fully blown bend. They put me in a chamber, gave me oxygen to wash the symptoms away and then I carried on with decompression as normal.

There was also another, less lethal, form of the bends.

When we had been selected to dive, the superintendent would tell us who was going into saturation and who wasn't. There would always be a couple of grim faces.

Basically, the divers doing the work would get about £1,000 per day, whereas the standby divers got about £400 per day. On each job there would always have to be two standby sat divers on the vessel. If they didn't get selected to go into sat, as opposed to getting near £30,000 for the days, they would get nearer £10,000. Don't get me wrong, bloody good money, but compared to the others on a grand a day, nowhere near as good. This was coined the 'financial bends'.

With the product lifecycle of a sat diver being limited, we liked to do up to 150 days a year if possible, some even more. An unorthodox and physically risky, yet financially effective method to gain more work, was to have two diving log books. By showing you had rested enough in one book, you could squeeze the odd sneaky week in here and there. I didn't do it myself, but it was common practice among many in the industry.

Back to the chambers.

For the next 28 days, they are home. Food, clean clothes, and anything else we required was sent in from outside via a medical lock. During our time in that chamber, there were a few things which would remind us that we were in a pressurised environment. Sometimes when we least expected it.

Once, I asked for some HP sauce which duly arrived with the food. My diving buddy was vigorously shaking the bottle, as you do with a new bottle of sauce, when there was a loud bang. I thought, 'Holy shit, what's gone wrong!' I looked at my mate to see brown sauce running down his face. The lad who'd sent the bottle had forgotten to loosen the lid and the bottle had imploded. We had to send out some soiled laundry along with the broken bottle. The opposite would have happened if we'd have sent out a tightened bottle through the lock – it would have exploded. The thought had passed my mind on a few occasions.

The divers who were in the chambers were looked after by saturation control (hereafter referred to as 'sat control'). This was staffed by a couple of life support technicians (LSTs), who were ably assisted by a tender who did all the legwork and took all the shit if things went wrong.

Sat control was the heartbeat of the chambers. It monitored the environment ensuring the correct gas mixture and temperature was maintained. They were instrumental to the divers' wellbeing and keeping the dive operation running smoothly. They were also the guys who did the final decompression. All of them were trained paramedics and could deal with most things. To say their role was vital would be an understatement. Lives depended on their competence.

If the whole thing turned to rats there was an emergency evacuation chamber on the deck that could accommodate all the divers and evacuate them to safety. This was all done at working pressure (the same pressure it was down in the saturation chambers).

Finally, there was dive control. This was the centre of the entire operation and where the dive supervisor controlled what happened during his 12-hour shift. He controlled the launch and recovery of the diving bell and was responsible for the divers' safety at all times. He had communications with the bridge of the vessel and the deck and talked directly with the crane. In essence, he was the hub of the operation, and as always, assisted by the aforementioned.

The supervisor would normally have been in the dive control or there would have been an engineer for the project close at hand and a company rep who would have an office next door with communications from the diver. He could listen to every word that was said, which kept them in the loop. The supervisor would now take control of the dive.

Diving companies are essentially contractors which means they have to be as efficient as possible. We mostly did fixed price work so the operations had to be slick, particularly as diving vessels were so expensive to hire.

In those days the computers and reference systems of the Dive Positioning (DP) boats were simply not as capable as they are today.

Nowadays the DP systems pretty much guarantee your position irrespective of bad weather, and are anchor free, due to the DP system motoring away to keep you on your desired coordinates. In fact, they are so reliable that the big North Sea platforms often have hotel platforms alongside, which are controlled using a DP system. In essence a floating hotel.

One thing hasn't changed over the years though – if conditions are so bad that a DP system or an anchor is struggling to keep you in your desired position, that's a good indication to call the dive off.

When an 'anchor up' vessel arrived at a work site, it used to take 12–18 hours to drop all its anchors and the same amount of time to pull them in when they'd finished the job. If they had to relocate at different parts of a platform, they had to go through the same process again and again – very time consuming. They also needed an anchor-handling tug with them, sometimes two.

The anchors were gigantic and each link on the chain weighed about 350lb (approximately 25st) and were about three feet wide. When you let one down, there would be a mass of smoke and rust flying off everywhere. You made sure you were nowhere near at the time. As the DP boats had no anchors, they could arrive on location and have a guy down and working in the water in less than an hour. No anchors to drag over pipelines and other subsea equipment, plus they were easily manoeuvrable and could work close by platforms. In some circumstances they could even have a gang plank to the platform.

The ones used for diving needed four reference systems (GPS) that fed information back to the computers. Similar to your car's sat nav, you would just take a fix and it would tell the computer where you were. The computer, in turn, would tell the vessel to stay put.

The second reference system was a surface radar, which was a line-of-sight system. Two radar antennas would look at each other and feed the information to the computer which would tell the vessel to stay put.

The third reference system was called a taut wire. This is a wire which goes down to the sea bed and is held on the sea bed by a weight which keeps the wire taut. The computer works out the angle of the wire and can tell the vessel to stay put.

The fourth and final system which could be used was an acoustic system. This is an underwater transponder which would send up a beep to the computer, in essence telling the computer what to do. As reference systems go, it was not the best because you got a lot of noise in the water caused mainly by the vessel thrusters. Even a shoal of fish swimming by could cause a signal failure.

We used three reference signals in case one of the three failed so, in theory, we could lose two systems and still maintain position. If all three went, the captain, or one of the DP operators, had to do the best they could manually; this was known as an emergency because it happened so quickly. The first thing they would know about it would be a loud alarm from the computer and a shudder as you hit the platform. The computer room had the same three computers all on lines and was capable of taking over if one failed.

The guy who controlled all of this was known as the DP operator and worked on the bridge. There were normally two of them in case one failed, or one had to make a cup of tea for the other. The DP console was staffed 24 hours a day. In the early days, when DP boats arrived on the scene, they only had one reference system. This caused a fair few dents to the platforms and resulted in several angry calls from the platform manager.

They used to get so angry, that they'd send us away to the 500-metre zone to standby until the captain could prove he had the ship under control. If you were in saturation at the time and were diving from the diving bell, your only way up was to go back to the bell, seal the bottom door, and let the lads on the surface recover the bell and lock it on to the dive system so they could transfer you to the main chambers.

It was a bit irresponsible but if the bell run was going on and on, we would cover the transponder with tin foil so the bridge would lose the signal and the dive abort alarm would go off in dive control. When the abort alarms sounded in dive control, the dive supervisor would press the button to speak and all you could hear in your helmet were the bells ringing. You'd have to haul your arse back to the bell which, when you looked towards it, was rapidly disappearing into the gloom. In the early days this was something I witnessed on a number of occasions.

One of the first things I learnt was to ensure my umbilical back to the bell was always clear of obstructions. Think of the consequences if I'd managed to take a turn round a bracing or some other obstruction. If my umbilical cord would have snapped and I'd have lost sight of the bell, that would have been that – early bath.

Running after the bell was fun so long as I didn't trip over. Divers never wore fins as seen on the television – they wore yellow wellies. I could run faster than I could swim and my feet stayed warmer in wellies filled with hot water. Checking one's umbilical became second nature after a while. If you did the tin foil trick you made sure you were sat under the bell, as there were simply no other options of where to go otherwise.

It was yet another steep learning curve in my aquatic life, but I was relishing anything and everything the future held for me.

12

Chamber Life

I GOT lucky with my first saturation trip with the new company. Normally you had to do a month on the surface getting used to the diving system. On this occasion they were having trouble burning the end of a pipeline off. Turns out some of the other divers had also told a few white lies about their underwater burning abilities.

Always a danger those wee white lies.

Underwater burning is a skill you don't learn in five minutes. Fortunately, back in Nigeria, I'd learnt how to burn in pitch black water. Despite a few near death experiences, I knew my time out there would come in useful at some point.

In those days there were only two divers in the bell at any one time. The person you were paired with was known as your bell partner. Once again, it turned out I was lucky as I ended up with a guy called Mike. Mike was ex-SAS – tough little chap. Very quiet though. Then again, I figured you probably didn't have to say much in the SAS. We dived together for a couple of years.

On this particular day we were told to get ready and go down to sat control which was where we'd be blown down using the decompression chamber. After a quick call to the wife to let her know what was happening – and that she'd have to write me a letter as I'd be out of contact for a month – off we went.

Mike had been into saturation once before so he knew the ropes. I just followed him.

I took a few clothes and a couple of books, then got into the chamber, shut the door behind us and waited. A speaker in the chamber asked if the door was shut and locked. Mike told them, 'Yes.' The speaker then said they'd blow us down to a depth of 30 feet and that we were stopping, so we could check for leaks. Down we went. With no leaks, Mike told them to go for it and to blow us down to the holding depth of around 200 feet, which would take a couple of hours. It's a good idea to equalise your ears on the way down. They like to blow you down slowly so your body gets used to being under pressure.

I laid on the bunk after only an hour or so thinking, 'Am I really going to live in a little chamber for a month?' The prospect started to feel like a long time. That said, I was committed, so there was no turning back.

As we started to descend into the murky depths (although it was probably a bit too late at that point) I did hope that I wouldn't suffer from claustrophobia as that would have been a nightmare situation. I started to think, 'Perhaps I should have thought a little bit longer before getting into the chamber, or perhaps even telling a few white lies to get the job in the first place.' It was too late now as we had almost reached depth.

On reaching depth, the door to the chamber opened to reveal where I would be living for the next month. The air wasn't stale, just bland.

The other divers were sitting there looking at us with big smiles. For them, the ordeal was over as they walked out. As I walked in, mine had just begun.

As we walked through, we said our hellos in our best Donald Duck voices and swapped places with the other two who had just finished their stint, and let them into our chamber – which is where they would start their four-day decompression. Simple really – so far, anyway. The diving bell had just left the chamber and would be gone for the next eight hours. The other two divers were asleep in another chamber. We had a quick chat with the two departing divers and they told us they'd been having trouble cutting the pipe.

It was a 36-inch pipe with a concrete coating. They'd knocked off the concrete, so it should have been relatively straightforward. They'd had about five dives trying but still hadn't managed to cut it in two.

Underwater burning is a knack. It's like when you see a plumber putting silicone around the bath in one perfect line and thickness, without a single bump. You then try it yourself and it looks like a caterpillar. Same with these guys burning.

We were going to give it a go next. I told them I was a good burner which, in all fairness, I was.

We sorted ourselves out and decided we'd go to the sleeping chamber and try and get some shut-eye before our dive. The two lads who'd just left had made up the beds with clean sheets, which was standard protocol. Find things as you left them.

Mike got the bottom bunk and I got the top one, which I soon discovered was pretty cramped – about six inches between me and the chamber wall. 'Great, a month of this!'

Then, the speaker on the wall came on again saying what would soon become our least favourite sentence, 'Next two divers, get ready.'

The other two divers grunted and rolled over. Mike and I made our way back to the main chamber to order breakfast. On the outside they were getting our diving equipment ready.

We finished breakfast, put the dirty dishes back in the medical lock, and were getting into our diving suits when the bell came back and was being locked on to the dive system. Transfer from the bell to the chamber is probably the riskiest part of the procedure. The flange on the top of the chamber has a big rubber ring so that, when the bell flange sits on it, it forms a seal. This seal is vital and must be checked for damage prior to any transfer.

Once the two flanges are together they're locked with a clamp with big tightening bolts. There's a short bit of trunking from the top of the chamber which is the same size as the door in the bell which you get in and out of. In the chamber was a door which swung downwards and a door in the bell that lifted up. Once the supervisor was happy that the mating procedure, as it was referred to, had been done properly, the trunking was pressurised until the door in the chamber swung down. You'd have to make sure you were not standing under the door at this point as it was extremely heavy. Deadly heavy in fact.

In the bell, the divers opened a valve on the bottom door which let the whole thing equalise. Now you'd have the bell and chamber at the same pressure, the bottom door of the bell could be lifted using a small winch. This door was also extremely heavy.

Once the bell door was opened, it was not unusual to have a huge dollop of water fall into the chamber below. This is why the chamber was known as the 'wet chamber'. Though this may sound like quite a complex procedure, it's not. You just had to follow the sequence of events which, all in all, only took about ten minutes.

The two divers came down out of the bell, bringing all their stuff with them including a Sodasorb Canister which was changed after every dive. It was used to scrub the gas in the bell so we didn't get a CO_2 build-up. Too much CO_2 in the bell would send the bell man to sleep – perhaps into a permanent one.

The atmosphere (air that is, not between divers – although that was also often tested to its limits) in the bell was constantly monitored from the surface but there were special tubes that could be used in the bell.

Once the bell was clear, the next diver who was staying in the bell did the checks. It was just routine stuff like checking the on-board emergency gas, the gas supply to the divers' masks, checking that the comms were working. If the checks weren't done, the bell might get to the bottom, not work properly and have to be recovered and fixed which would have been time consuming, so it was best to have everything done properly from the outset.

Mike was bell man on this dive. As I've said, I was a good burner and was happy to be first out into the water, which was not a bad idea really, seeing as it was my first saturation dive ever and it would be over quicker as opposed to dwelling on what the experience ahead could hold.

Bell checks over, I got the signal to go up and join Mike. The guys in the chamber pushed the door up and locked it with the latch. We lowered the door in the bell, closed the valve on the door, then opened the blow-down valve in the bell and put just enough pressure in the bell to make a seal on the bell door.

The dive supervisor opened a valve in the dive shack and let the pressure out of the small trunking between the bottom of the bell and the top of the chamber. Once he was happy, the chamber and bell were sealed and he released the rest of the gas from the trunking, unlocked the clamp, and the bell was ready for the launch procedure.

Launching the bell was fairly straightforward. It was held in a big frame which trolleyed across to the moon pool and was clamped to a couple of guide wires to stop it spinning. Released from the frame, it banged and clattered through the moon pool and out of the bottom of the ship into the open water below the boat.

You couldn't see anything from the bell. It did have a couple of small portholes but they were normally covered with the diver's umbilical.

When you had all the necessary equipment in the bell, things suddenly got much 'tighter' so it was important you and your bell partner liked one another. Down we went, until we got to the same pressure in the water as it was in the chamber. Then the bottom door bubbled open, indicating that the seal had been broken and we were on the bottom. The door was lifted with the winch and clipped into the open position.

Normally the bell man would hit the blowdown valve again and put more gas in the bell. This would just lower the level of water in the bell trunking, keeping the floor of the bell dry. You don't want wet feet if you're sitting there for eight hours.

Once the door was open, it was time to get the diver dressed. You helped him put his helmet, hot water suit and gloves on, and plugged his hot water supply into the side of his suit. Once this was done, the diver slipped out of the bottom door of the bell on to the clump weight below the bell. He'd stay here, have a comms check with the surface, and would get himself orientated and happy with his gas supply and hot water.

He'd then ask the surface to 'slack the diver's umbilical'. The surface would relay this to the man in the bell. The guy in the bell couldn't talk directly to the diver in the water. When he was happy with his slack, off he went to the work site.

The diver in the bell would be fully dressed without his helmet on ready to leave the bell if the man in the water got into any trouble. This one was only going to get into trouble if he couldn't burn the pipe off.

I found the pipe that was in the process of being cut. It had so many pop holes from where the previous divers had had a go at it with their burning torch, that it looked like a kitchen colander. I had a good look at the cut and decided it would be easier for me to start a completely fresh cut. The dive supervisor wasn't a happy bunny when I told him. I guess he had the company man sitting next to him, but for me, it was going to be the easiest way. They agreed, so I started cutting pipe.

When a pipe is sat on the sea bed you cut down both sides as far as you can, then you have to cut a big window in the side big enough to get your arm in so you can cut the bottom half from the inside. After my four hours were up, I cut the top and made the window. I thought Mike could have the glory and finish it off, so I went back to the bell for the swap over. In those days you were only meant to do four hours in the water, but you could get dispensation to do longer. These days, the guys from Health and Safety wouldn't even dream about letting a diver go a minute over the allocated time.

I took my helmet off and told Mike how far we'd got. He leant over to me and whispered, 'I can't burn.'

It turned out they don't teach you how to do an underwater burn in the SAS. I remember thinking at least he'll come in handy if we have a terrorist attack.

I told the supervisor that I'd prefer to finish what I had started. Mike gave me a little smile. I had a drink of water and put my helmet back on.

I probably could have done with using the loo quickly, but held on knowing it was not a long job. Worst case scenario, I would take a pee in my diving suit if the job overran. Perk of the job.

I've often been asked what would happen if I needed to take a number two while down there. In all honesty, this rarely happens. In fact, in all the years I dived, I've never heard of anyone needing to go. That said, if you had an undercooked chicken vindaloo for dinner in the chamber and two hours into your shift it decided it wanted out, there'd be no option but to take a dump in your suit.

Anyway – back to this burning job. Three and a half hours later it was finished. I've never been so happy as when I took that helmet off. It took about an hour for my face to get anything like back to normal. Those oral nasals could deform, what normally was, quite a handsome face.

We stowed the gear, shut the bottom door, and started the recovery process. It'd been a good start to my new job – I'd cut a pipe and made a new friend.

Once you'd been up and down a few times, it got easier. After a couple of weeks, the end was in sight. However, those weeks being confined in a small space came with their own challenges.

13

Nowhere To Run

AS the atmosphere was quite humid in the chamber, it was an ideal breeding environment for bacteria, and it was very possible to pick up some nasty infections. Despite using silica gel to help purify the air and keep the moisture out, there were always people suffering from some chamber related ailments. Bad ear syndrome was quite common in those days. Not sure if that's an official term, but it's how we referred to this excruciatingly painful fungus that would develop in one ear and quickly transfer to the other. Between the humidity and any change in pressure, it was just horrible. A diving bell was certainly not the best place to be. They used to give you aluminium acetate to help prevent it, then Otosporin to cure it.

One guy came out in over 60 boils, but nobody knew why. Again, probably to do with the humidity, but again, not ideal in that environment. We steered clear from him like a leper.

Neck rub was another common problem. The rubber seal which went around your neck used to rub all the skin off and, because of the humid environment, it'd never heal. When your neck's raw, salt water stings like mad. With some of the guys, it got so bad they had to be decompressed early. That used to really piss their bell partners off as they had to go with them, seriously hurting their wealth in the process.

A chamber was also not the place to have a heart attack. Not that you would want to have a heart attack in any particular place, but you'd prefer to have it somewhere where it didn't take you four days to get decompressed. Having a heart attack down in the chamber was pretty much a death sentence.

The other bad thing was if something happened to a friend or relative as you couldn't just get out and go home. The diver and diving partner would have to be decompressed before being allowed to see their loved ones.

There were a couple of incidents of this nature. One of the divers' wives had been killed in a car crash. The poor guy had to be sedated on hearing the news. The four days in decompression must have seemed like the longest of his life.

Comms in general were very slow. The only system you had was to talk to the dive supervisor in the shack, through a little squawk box radio on the wall. You would press a button which set off an alarm in his chamber and he'd ask what you wanted. It didn't help with the helium as the further you went down, the squeakier you became. Despite the use of voice synthesisers, we were pretty tough to understand.

Thankfully comms underwater were much better. Certainly far better than I'd experienced previously. In my original days of air diving, comms was basically a pull on the rope attached to me. One pull would be a check to see if I was okay, two pulls would be to say I'd be coming up in five minutes, which I'd respond to by giving two pulls back to confirm. Three pulls was to say my time under was up and I needed to surface.

When I started saturation diving, I was on comms all the time – voice comms. For sat diving, the tug of a rope simply wouldn't have been good enough as the complexity of the commands for the tasks required needed two-way dialogue. Tugging twice on a rope to say you were not okay would not give reasons why and there was no option to pull you to the surface due to decompression.

In terms of keeping you up to date with current affairs in the chamber – forget it. Once a week, when the supply boat came out with the crew change, they'd have newspapers and that would be your contact with the outside world. No radio, no TV and certainly no internet. Consequently, the culture is somewhat different to what it is now. In my days you could in effect have solitude for a month – now, with wifi in the chamber, there's no hiding place from the likes of e-mail and Skype. Although I'm sure those in the chamber have worked out how to show the comms are not working when they need to have a break.

The mail also used to come once a week. It wasn't unusual for someone to get a Dear John letter. This really used to get them going. I remember, once, asking this Scot if he ever worried about his wife being unfaithful to which he replied, 'Anyone who'd fuck my wife is too lazy to masturbate.'

That's that then, I thought.

When it came to breaking the news of the death of loved ones, they had a strange way of telling you such things when you were in the saturation chamber. The dive supervisor would come on the comms and say, 'All those with a mother put your hand up.' Hands would all go up. Then he would say, 'Put your hand down Smith,' and the other lads in the chamber would say to Smith, 'Sorry to hear about your loss.' Black humour was almost part of the package you signed up for as a diver.

Between the main chamber and the sleeping chamber was the wet chamber, with the trunking that led to the bell. The wet chamber was home to the toilet.

Going to the toilet when you were in saturation was an art and you had to follow the procedures.

First, you sat down and did whatever. Once you'd finished, you would stand up and stamp on the pedal to let things out. You would then tell surface you'd finished. They'd in turn send someone down, who would open a valve on the outside to remove it into a holding tank on the outside.

There was an American guy working on a different job who had a very nasty experience. He was still sitting on the pot when someone opened the valve on the outside – it sucked his insides out. The lads cruelly joked that at least he was no longer full of shit. The medics had to literally take his colon and push it all back up again. He was lucky to survive.

You really had to learn to follow the procedures. Now, they watch your every movement on the TV. That's all right until the vessel goes into a port which is when they let people look around. Let's just say the well-endowed would receive lots of letters from the secretaries.

When I was diving, they didn't have too many Norwegian divers but the ones they did have weren't particularly good, so they tried to make the English guys dive with a Norwegian. This went down like a lead balloon and we'd do anything to get out of it.

One of the boys used to lay on his bunk and wank for Britain. This used to really aggravate the Norwegians who'd call up to the surface and ask the supervisor to tell the English diver to stop doing it in front of him. The conversation would go a bit like this, 'Bob, we've had a complaint about your behaviour. Would you stop doing what you're doing in front of the other guy?' The answer was always, 'No.'

It reached the point where they'd end up having a punch-up in the bell. Shortly after that, it was back to your old bell partners. I suppose it was one method of getting your own way.

Ultimately, you would go down into the chamber with the guy you would dive with, but it was a lottery as to who else you would be sharing the chamber with. There's certainly been some colourful characters over the years several hundred feet below the surface.

Christmas was always fun in the chambers. You were even allowed a small glass of wine. 'Ho ho ho, what fun!' We'd put streamers up, open our cards and wish each other happy Christmas. We couldn't wait for lunch, which frankly, tasted the same as every other meal, due to the helium, which made everything flavourless. Normally, when the menu used to come down and you chose say beef, fish or turkey, the only way you could tell your choice was correct was by looking at it. I used to think, 'It looks like fish, so it will taste like fish (or beef etc.).' The reality is, if I ate blindfolded, I could have been eating cat food and wouldn't have known.

Christmas lunch was immediately followed by eight hours in the water. Remember – they pay saturation divers well, and if you were down there for 28 days, that meant 28 dives. Nobody ever dressed up as Father Christmas – although that might have looked amusing to other divers on the sea bed. Perhaps a niche for new generations of Christmas divers?

We used to look forward to our time in the water as it was like a day out. You got a little time to yourself – well, you and the fish.

If you've never lived in close confinement for 28 days, you might not appreciate how things can get on your nerves. Even little things used to drive me mad – leaving a wet towel lying about or an empty cup on the table. Listening to someone fart. The sound of someone cleaning their bowl with a spoon to get the last morsel of food from it, could drive a man to violent crime!

We only had one Norwegian guy go a bit funny. His wife sent him a picture of her new boyfriend – his best mate.

The diving thankfully acted as your opportunity to get away from the madness in the chamber and also kept you fit. As opposed to astronauts who have to exercise while in outer space, in order to avoid muscle waste, divers, although also cooped up in a small chamber, would probably come back fitter than they went in – and that had nothing to do with exercising in the chamber. When you work with heavy tools for about ten hours per day, with each motion being far heavier than it normally would as a result of the water slowing you down, you have no option but to become fit.

When the 28 days were over and it was my turn to decompress, it almost seemed like a relief. Subconsciously, I must have controlled myself while I was in there, but once I started decompression, I couldn't wait to get out. That made four days in decompression seem like a long time.

One thing I certainly remembered on that first decompression session, was how important it was for my teeth to be in good shape. After a couple of hours of being in the chamber, one of my fillings blew off. Thankfully for me, when it blew off there was no pain, just a hole left where the filling used to sit. Unfortunately, some of my mates had a crown blow, which took part of the tooth and gum with it. Painful stuff to have to endure for the next three days. If a tooth is decayed below the filling and air is locked into that space, during decompression it will blow off. I made a note to myself to be a regular at the dentist.

The decompression chamber had no washing or toilet facilities, just a dustbin with a black bin liner. When you cleaned your teeth, you spat the water in the bag that you'd just urinated in. It used to make your eyes water a bit. There was an unwritten rule that you could wee in the bag but not poo. This was not easy.

One night I woke up and found Mike sat on the bin. I shouted, 'No, no!' 'I'm not, I'm not!' he said.

I don't think he did but it must have been close.

Thankfully, when it came to the toilet, you didn't really get to smell anything until the door opened when decompression was over.

A funny thing happens when the door opens and the air comes in – your voice goes from Donald Duck to a deep, resonant sound in a matter of seconds. You think, 'Is that really me? I sound like one of those Shakespearean actors.'

Something else you notice when you sit down for your first meal on the boat is that your tastebuds go through the roof. It sounds silly, but everything tasted natural again.

After decompression you had to stay around for 24 hours to make sure you were not going to get the bends. That was the last thing you wanted when you were going home next day, especially as you only had one thing on your mind.

My time on a particular Norwegian boat in 1977 came to a sudden end, when I was asked to go into saturation with this particular Norwegian. I didn't like him which made it worse.

It was just after Christmas. We were having lunch on the boat – a really good spread with plenty of fish. In the middle of the table was a pig's head with an apple in its mouth.

I was sat next to the superintendent who wanted me to dive with this Norwegian guy. I was trying to get out of it and dive with my new mate, Frank. He kept asking why I wouldn't dive with him so I told him his English was terrible and I wouldn't feel safe in an emergency. He said his English was fine.

I called over to the Norwegian diver and asked him a question to which he mumbled something incoherent. I'd just asked if he could take the apple out of the pig's mouth.

He let me and Frank dive together after that.

We both got the letter on the same day while we were on leave: company policy states that, if required, you must dive with a Norwegian diver – apple or no apple.

Thank you and goodbye.

14

Becoming A Grown-Up

IN 1978 came the end of my getting-wet days. No more bad ears, no more prune-like skin or being immersed for 12 hours in hot salt water and having my head stuck in a helmet with an oral nasal clamped over my nose which pushed my eyes into a slit – not the most comfortable way to spend a day. Not to mention being locked up for 28 days in a floating prison and walking around the ocean floor talking to fish. I was officially no longer a diver.

The timing was good as my wife had just given birth to our beautiful daughter in 1977 and baby number two was soon on his way – so I decided to have some time off. That was until I got a phonecall from my mate saying a new company had just started up which was looking for superintendents. The job in brief meant being in charge of the diving system on the boat, ensuring the job in hand was completed competently.

Apparently, he'd put our names forward. He had less experience than me and I was far from qualified for this job. They must have been desperate as we got the jobs and a whole new era started for me. Although I was still based around the perils of the sea, I was spending more time looking down at it, as opposed to looking up from the bottom of the ocean.

We got a new vessel called the *Northern Protector*. It was not brand-new, but new to us. Along with the vessel we also got new dive and marine crews who were still learning how to work a DP system, which was new to everyone at the time within the diving industry.

In those days, if you worked for Occidental Petroleum Ltd you got a lot of Americans helping you – if 'help' is the right word. The company reps were all American ex-divers; nothing like 20 years of diving in the swamps of Louisiana to set you up for the North Sea.

As for a boat that didn't have anchors, it was a stretch for those guys. But off we went to Piper Alpha – this was about ten years before it blew up. Though we did pass Piper Beta which had just been destroyed by fire.

Getting permission to come close to the platform and start diving was an experience. The captain who was in charge of the boat and its safety acted like he was conducting an orchestra. We were all banished to the wing of the bridge and warned to remain absolutely quiet while the maestro did his bit. I think even the computer had trouble understanding him. He kept looking at his gauges and shouting to the other officers on the bridge, 'Split! Give me the split!'

It was something to do with the power level to the thrusters. Eventually we settled down long enough for him to give us the go-ahead to dive.

I don't think he had much confidence in the system to start with – he wanted an open comms line to the dive shack just in case we had a run off and hit the platform.

After that, things went well. The diving was okay and the boat never hit the platform. One of the divers reported he'd found a body which caused quite a commotion. It turned out to be a pig's carcass. God knows how it got there.

As confidence grew on the bridge we were allowed to get nearer to the magic computer. One day, I was talking to the captain, leaning on the console and shooting the shit when *crunch* – my elbow had gone right through one of the thruster gauges.

'Split! Give me the split!' The captain went white with rage. I, too, figured it was time to split.

One night I was in dive control and the weather was marginal, while my nerves were on edge. The bell hydraulics were broken and I couldn't recover the bell. Our mechanic was fixing it. Not a big problem he said, just a couple of minutes. We were recovering the bell early because the hot water machines had broken down and the weather was still picking up.

On the previous dive, one of the divers had refused to leave the bell when it was his turn in the water. Turns out he was terrified and had lost his nerve completely. In that situation there's nothing else for it but to get him and his bell partner into decompression as quick as possible and get him out of there. It was a right screw-up at the beginning of a saturation dive as you would lose a chamber while they decompressed. I wasn't very pleased as I found out afterwards that he'd been feeling apprehensive before he went in but thought he'd be okay. Having anxiety or a sense of claustrophobia before going into a chamber is a terrible thing. He had both and more.

Just then I noticed the platform was drifting past. That's strange, I thought.

I called the bridge and asked if we were moving. The answer was beyond belief.

'What are you doing calling at a time like this?' said the captain. 'Don't you know we're out of control?'

'Why haven't you pushed the fucking dive abort button then?!' I replied.

Luckily for the lads in the bell, we were drifting away from the platform and into open water as opposed to straight into the platform, so no harm came.

Once we'd got the bell back and the lads were safe I called the company rep and captain and said, 'Take me back to Aberdeen. We need to get this thing fixed.'

'That's a big decision, boy,' said the American rep.

'Not from where I am standing, it isn't,' I replied.

'You might never work for Occidental again,' he said.

'Three weeks ago I'd never even heard of Occidental,' I responded.

Suffice to say, after Piper Alpha blew up I never heard of them again.

That was my first trip as a superintendent. I remember thinking, things can only get better. The guy who was shift supervisor that night was a guy called Keith. He looked just like Dick Emery. He spent every spare minute researching and trying to sell an idea to whoever would listen to him that there was £45m of gold to be had for anyone willing to risk it all on a salvage expedition. The ship in question was the HMS *Edinburgh*, which had been sunk in 1942 by the Germans in the icy Barents Sea.

Our company (Wharton Williams) took the bait and at the end of 1981 recovered the £45m 800 feet below the surface. After they had given a cut to the Russians, because it was on their turf, and a nice drink to Keith, Wharton Williams still yielded enough cash to be able to put a deposit on two ships – *Deepwater 1* and *Deepwater 2*. When Rockwater took over the company at a later date, the boats were renamed *Rockwater 1* and *Rockwater 2* and then swiftly nicknamed *Rocky 1* and *Rocky 2*. Funnily enough, at the time of writing this book, my brother is currently a manager on one of the boats in Singapore!

Recovering that kind of cash can put a smile on your face. At a later date I'd also be involved with treasure hunting of my own.

15

O Is For Oblivion

WE were on a job for Brown and Root at the Shearwater Aquamarine in the North Sea around 1981, in which the water was about 60 feet deep. This was pretty shallow for these boats as about 30 feet of the hull rested below the surface of the water. However, they still operated perfectly well.

The problem for a diver is that the thrusters do make a lot of noise and at 60 feet they feel as though they're right on top of you.

The other issue with having a boat so shallow, was increasing the likelihood of sending the ROVs to an early grave.

The ROV is a piloted camera with a big light, kind of like aqua big brother, which was used to film divers when they were working. The reps used them to check we were doing things correctly, but when we first started using the ROVs, we treated them like spies. After a while we respected their merits. It was like having another pair of eyes when we were looking for something and they could add light to a situation we might not have otherwise seen. From being an enemy, the ROVs became our little friends.

However, with a shallow setting, it had been known for them to come to an abrupt ending as it was possible for them to get caught in the suction of the thrusters. Try as they may, their little thrusters were no match for the barge thrusters and there was only ever going to be one winner. It would be a slow death which the ROV filmed. His little thrusters frantically going backwards at full revs as the blades of the vessel thrusters get bigger and bigger. Then blackness and it was all over.

The operators would then rush outside the control hut looking over the side for their beloved little friend to pop up in one piece.

Sometimes the wait was long and gave them hope, but then up popped little bits of red or yellow floatation and they knew it was over. The guys looked away with tears in their eyes as their beloved mechanical baby was no longer. It was a bit of a nuisance really because it took six hours to get the spare into the water.

Suffice to say, air divers working on these vessels were wary of succumbing to the same fate.

On this particular job, our boat was a saturation boat in full DP mode but we were air diving from it. Our normal saturation diving crew hated air diving (it was like playing in the second division in the Football League) so we used air divers or unqualified gas divers. Sat divers were, and still are, the guys who make the money – after all, they're risking life and limb.

Jobs like this were good for air divers trying to get their gas ticket. They had to do a certain number of air dives before they could go forward for their gas ticket. From memory I think it was about 100 air dives needed and £30,000.

Listening to air divers working always scared the shit out of me. They'd breathe so fast and it was so noisy because they were blowing bubbles all the time. All you could hear was air rushing round inside their helmets. It was as if they couldn't draw breath fast enough. Saturation divers were quiet and managed to get the job done in a more tranquil, bubble-free setting.

The air dive station was always in the middle of the ship, so as to be as far away from those thrusters as possible. The diver always went down in an air dive basket lowered by a winch protruding over the edge of the boat. His umbilical was fed down from the surface and kept tight. When he reached the bottom and was ready to exit the basket, he did so keeping his umbilical tight; there should never be any slack umbilical floating about for the thrusters to grab.

There was always a standby diver sitting on the surface fully dressed, ready to jump in, just in case of an emergency. Sometimes the standby diver would go down in the dive basket with the diver just to tend his umbilical.

The dive supervisor on this job was a mate of mine called Bill, who had a bit of a stutter, and was consequently known to everyone as 'Stuttering Bill'.

We were on location and the vessel had stabilised. Stabilisation is part of the vessel set-up. They get on location, set all their references for the DP then let the computer do its thing. They then monitor everything for about 20 minutes and if everything is okay you get the green light.

The light system was just like traffic lights: green for go, orange for standby or get the diver back to the bell (or basket if you were in the middle of a dive), and red meant it's all gone to rat shit so get everyone back as soon as possible and recover them to the surface. Red was normally when you had a DP boat run off course and the vessel was not fully under control.

We had the green light and the young diver was ready. Stuttering Bill gave the order to dive and the launch procedure got under way. The basket swung over the side, the order to lower the basket was given, and down the diver went.

The diver would always say in a loud voice, 'Leaving the surface,' which indicated the start of their dive time. His depth was always monitored from the surface and we would stop them five or six feet from the bottom. The basket got to the bottom and was stopped. The diver would get himself orientated, find the work site and then get cracking. On this particular day, we were looking at a pipeline that was meant to have some damage caused by something which had been dragged over it.

The visibility in the water was non-existent so the diver had to grovel about the bottom, walking round in circles until he fell over the pipe. Not very scientific, but it worked. As these boats were so accurate with the DP set-up, you were nearly always right over where you needed to be.

The diver left the basket and started wandering round. He reported shortly after that he'd found the pipe and was looking for damage.

I was walking past where Bill had the radio and could hear the diver talking to Bill. Everything seemed normal. I uttered a few sage words of wisdom to the deck crew along the lines of, 'Tidy the fucking deck up.'

On walking back I could hear water rushing about in the diver's helmet, which was not a great sign.

'What's going on Bill?' I asked.

Bill's stutter had gone when he replied in a panic, 'I can't contact the diver. It looks like he's bailed out. The water's rushing round in his helmet and he's not talking.'

I replied, 'You'd better jump the standby diver and find out what's going on then.'

The lads quickly put the standby diver's helmet on him. You could tell by his face he wasn't looking forward to this but that's what standby divers do in an emergency – and this was an emergency.

Over the side and down the basket wire he went, along the diver's umbilical, through the basket, and along to the end.

After what felt like an age he found the diver's helmet...but there was no sign of our lad.

He reported this all back to the surface. The atmosphere in the comms room was not great. We didn't know if he'd bailed out and perhaps was going to appear on the surface dead or alive. In the meantime the thrusters were belting away, keeping this boat in position in shallow water and I was starting to wonder if he was going through the thrusters. The truth is, all we had was an empty helmet to go by. These were anxious moments.

Bill told the standby diver to search around and see if he could find him. When he had no luck, he was told to recover the guy's diving helmet and return to the dive basket ready for recovery. He returned to the basket and was recovered to the surface.

Remember the old saying: panic kills.

Bailing out under a dive boat in shallow water with its thrusters roaring away is always a high risk strategy.

The guys on the deck were looking over the side to see if the diver popped up. We figured something must have happened to make him bail out.

I had this image of him coming close to a thruster then being sucked through and getting the same treatment as an ROV.

I was listening for a graunching noise or a change in tone from the thrusters but none came. It makes you feel sick just thinking about it. Whatever made him do it?

The vessels always had an inflatable safety craft for an emergency and on this particular occasion they were told to launch it in case the diver came up away from the boat. God knows which way the tide was running. We looked all over, but the lad never came up.

Divers are meant to wear rubber suits under their hot water suits. This gives them buoyancy in the event of a free ascent, but they used to wear woolly bear drysuits under the hot water suits, because they said it was more comfortable. Problem with woolly bears is they had the buoyancy of a brick.

The diver's equipment was working fine when we checked it, so there didn't seem to be any reason for him to bail out – but bail out he obviously had.

It was at this time I found out the ship had lost position and shifted sideways. They said it was only a few feet but it later turned out to be several hundred feet.

Some of the diving crew had just come off a job a matter of weeks before, which this particular diver had been on. There had been an incident with a slack umbilical which had gone in the thruster and pulled the diver's helmet clean off his head. Luckily for him he was in the air dive basket and was able to hang on. I guess this was still fresh in his mind.

When our vessel lost position and went sideways his umbilical would have been tugged. Alarm bells would have gone off and he'd have been thinking 'here I go' so my guess is he bailed out, ditched his head gear and just stood there on the ocean floor. If he had let the boat drag him along he might still be here today. Who knows what you might do in the same situation? All I know is it takes eight minutes to drown.

He left a wife and a newborn baby. Awful.

When something like this happens all hell lets loose and you have to stop everything and call the Health and Safety Executive (HSE) so they can come and do an investigation. It's a crime scene until they've checked things and given you permission to go back to work.

Most diving companies had their own diving manual which incorporated an emergency section – this was ours.

We would call the beach on a ship-to-shore radio, as anyone listening to that channel could hear what was being said. Our manual had an alphabetical code that indicated how bad the accident had been: 'A' for a broken toenail and so on. Ours went all the way to 'O' for death.

I called the office to give them the news and asked to speak with the operations manager who was the top man in a situation like this.

The girl on the desk said he was in a meeting and asked if I could call back. I told her to tell him I had an 'O' situation. After a while she came back on the phone and told me he didn't know what I was talking about but he was going to his phone.

He comes on the phone all gruff and grumpy and asked me what I was on about. I explained I had an 'O' situation. He asked me if I'd been drinking. I said we have an 'O' and it's in the emergency manual.

'What's O stand for?' he said.

As I was beginning to lose the plot I came straight out and told him one of the divers has just drowned. He got the message and said in his best voice that he would handle everything from his end. Great. Now all we had to do was wait for everyone to turn up.

It was a good time to see what the captain had to say about things. If the vessel had lost position the dive abort alarm should have gone off, but it hadn't. We only knew the boat had moved out of position because the surveyor who sat on the bridge (who gave the position required manually via the transponders), turned to the DP operator and said the boat was out of position. The DP operator knew something was up and had called the captain to the bridge.

We had a mystery that had cost the life of a young diver and had to find out what had happened before we could even consider going back to work. The vessel was stable once again, everything was working fine. Once the vessel had its reference systems deployed and working, they normally used the acoustic transponder as a reference.

It was placed on the sea bed, where it returned a signal independent of the others.

When a boat moves too far away in any direction, the transponder should set off the alarms in the computer. Due to the depth in which we were operating, the taut wire system was the strongest system and the computer was using this as its main operating mode.

Before this incident it was common practice on this vessel to deploy the transponder on the taut wire weight. It wouldn't have taken a genius to work out that if anything went wrong with the taut wire system and it failed, your reference system would not work. It would go wherever the weight went, never giving the computer a signal that the boat was on the move.

This tragedy was unfortunately another learning curve that nobody wanted to see repeated.

Soon, the HSE guys arrived and were happy with the explanation. I knew one of the guys from a previous job. He was an old diver and understood the situation. Next to arrive was an American guy, who was one up from the operations manager. You either liked him or hated him. I liked him.

It was a typical 'show your face' visit. He arrived in a red helicopter with the standard issue survival suit which, when he peeled it off, revealed an immaculate grey suit.

Very James Bond.

I went to the helilounge to meet him and had a quick chat to bring him up to speed. This guy looked like the spitting image of Robert Redford. He came in with a big smile, hand outstretched, and the first words he said to me were, 'Hi, Dave. So, what are you doing these days, apart from killing divers?'

What a guy.

Later that day I found him in the mess room explaining to the other divers how the dead diver's wife would be much better off, now, because she'd be getting a load of insurance money.

In his own way he was saying she'd be looked after, as would any of the other diver's wives if they were to come to the same fate. I think that was lost on them as they were still in shock. Later on in my career they would send counsellors out but I preferred the American guy any day.

A year later, when they held the inquest in Hull, my boss called me up just before we convened and told me they'd found the guy's hot water suit. It had washed up on the Danish coast. The suit was empty. The sea had eaten him.

16

Fire In The Bell

A YEAR later, in 1982, I was faced with a new scenario, which provided me with yet another challenge.

Our client was Shell, and I was in charge of maintenance and inspection on board a vessel called *The Workhorse*, which was a vessel I was very familiar with and had just been done up. However, they could have saved the refurb as we were about to have a fire on board which ended up being quite nasty.

It all started when the dive engineer was filling the hot water machines with diesel. The hot water machines are what pump the hot water down to the diver's suit via an umbilical.

The umbilical goes down to the diving bell and in turn feeds hot water to the diver's suit. The suit's inner lining has a lot of pipes, like veins. These veins have little holes in them and the water sort of floods out of these holes and immerses the body in hot water at just the right temperature, controlled from the surface.

A diver's umbilical is only about 60 or 70 feet long, but if he loses hot water there's a good chance he won't make it back to the bell. If he does, he'll be very cold and in need of a cuddle.

This particular dive engineer had asked the engine room to start the diesel pumps to the deck, which they did. He was going round the three hot water pumps topping up the tanks and was now on the last one. They took several minutes to fill and the guy had gone to check something else and forgotten all about it. Diesel had overflowed from the tank and found its way to the burners which had ignited into a ball of fire. The overflowing diesel was flooding into the moon pool and floating on top of the water. The fire quickly spread and we now had a situation to deal with.

The moon pool is a round hole in the middle of the boat – it's what the diving bell goes through on its way into the water. It's in the middle of the boat as this is the area with the least amount of heave and pitch. It also makes it easier to launch and recover the bell.

The bell is lowered through the moon pool using a winch, and is clipped to two wires – one either side to stop it spinning. At the bottom of those two wires is a big weight which keeps everything else from spinning round. The bell umbilical comes from the top of the bell to another winch on the surface. This umbilical provides the diver's breathing gas, communications and hot water. If the umbilical is severed there's a back-up. The bell does carry emergency gas on board, but there's no means of heating the inside of the bell.

On this day, the divers were on the bottom working away when the fire in the moon pool burnt through the umbilical. The diving supervisor first noticed something was wrong when he lost contact with the bell. His dive control on this vessel was above and slightly to one side of the moon pool, which meant he could see the fire when he looked out of the dive control door.

He was horrified to see the flames leaping up as saturation control was starting to fill with smoke.

The senior LST had been told he should transfer the guys into the deck rescue chamber but not to launch it until we'd got the lads back who were trapped in the bell below.

Things were getting tricky and the fire was out of control and getting worse.

When the emergency communications to the bell cease to work, there is a back-up system called Through Water Communications. Suffice to say, it does what it says on the packet. To do this, you have to lower a transponder over the side. You lower it as far as you can until you get it into quiet water. The bell has another transponder on the top. The two transponders talk to each other and send the voices through the water. Only problem is, they never seem to work that well as you get a garbled message coming through. Not helpful at the best of times, but especially not during situations such as this.

The divers in the bell below noticed there was a problem when the surface-supplied gas went off and the divers' hot water stopped flowing. Luckily, the diver who was in the water wasn't far from the bell and got himself back and inside quickly. They then switched to on-board emergency gas and turned on their Through Water Comms.

At this time they would have had about 12 hours of gas left. Twelve hours seems a long time when you say it, but if you're 400 feet below the surface sitting in a diving bell that's stuck and the vessel you have to return to is on fire, it's not long at all.

The diving supervisor had done the Through Water Comms bit and told the divers to get in the bell, shut the bottom door ready for recovery and said, 'As soon as we have things under control, we'll recover the bell to the surface.' God knows how the divers in the bell must have felt. When you hear a message that says '…as soon as we have things under control…', human nature tends to remind you, at that moment in time, things are 'not' in control.

In saturation, the LST was getting the guys in the chambers ready to go through into the rescue chamber, when the one who'd been sent up to get it ready for launch came back down and gave some more bad news – the chamber was on fire. All the lads had to come back into the main chamber and shut the internal doors to isolate the rescue chamber in case it had to be jettisoned. This was not a good situation. There was a boat on fire, a rescue chamber on fire, and a bell with three divers stuck on the bottom of the North Sea.

It was getting so hot in sat control that the LSTs had breathing masks on and wet towels on their heads. Eventually they had to leave sat control as it was too dangerous to stay. One of the LSTs told the guys in the chamber what was happening, told them not to worry, that things would soon be under control and that they'd be back to the lock in time for their midday meal.

There were some anxious faces at the portholes as the guys left sat control. I quickly spoke to Stuttering Bill and asked if there was any message he wanted me to pass on to his wife. Although I was saying it with a slant of humour, the reality was that I was probably closer to having to pass on the message to his wife at this point as opposed to not.

The boat's crew was starting to get things moving especially as the fire had taken everyone by surprise. The dive supervisor had been forced to evacuate the dive control, leaving the divers on the bottom, without any contact to the outside world.

The diesel feeding the fire had been shut off in the engine room, so providing the fire didn't find an alternative means of fuel to keep it going, the ship's crew should have been able to get things under control. The sprinkler system was spraying away like mad and they had a hose showering down on the moon pool. It was an hour or so before things were good enough to re-enter sat control.

The LSTs soon calmed the divers in the chamber and promised to lock away the letters they'd all written to their loved ones just as soon as they'd finished reading them.

They must have all written a letter to their wives, girlfriends, or family and put them in the medical lock just in case the worst happened – the worst being the fire melted the rubber seals on the chamber doors. This would have caused what is known as 'explosive decompression'. Quite literally, the divers in the chamber would have disintegrated in an instant.

With the moon pool fire out, the dive supervisor was able to re-enter the dive shack. Through Water Comms was still hanging over the side and still working intermittently. The boys below were happy to hear his voice, as by this time they only had about two hours tops left in the tank. Recovery should have only taken ten minutes or so. The supervisor switched on the hydraulic bell recovery winch, only to find it didn't work as all the hoses had burned through. Not ideal. It would have taken several hours to change and repair all of the hoses but, as with most things on a dive system, there was a back-up.

On a bell recovery system, if the main winch fails the bell can be lifted using the main umbilical (not an option on this day). Option two involved the guide weight winch, which could lift the bell by means of bringing the weight up underneath it, lifting the whole lot in one go.

The winch was normally hydraulic but could also be operated using air. Air made it slow and wouldn't allow the bell and weight to be lifted out of the water. It would, however, have got the bell close enough for air divers to attach a surface rigged wire from an alternative winch. It would take time, but it was the best option we had while the mechanic worked on the main recovery winch.

Once we had the bell up into air diving range we could also run down an emergency umbilical which would fit on a special panel above the bell. This would at least give the guys hot water, as by now they would have been feeling the cold, as their only means of keeping warm was a space blanket kept in the bell survival kit. The emergency umbilical would also provide surface-supplied gas and comms. We just had to get them up into air dive range.

The whole process was painfully slow as the higher we got them, the heavier the bell got with the extra weight of the main bell wire. It reached the point where the auxiliary winch couldn't lift any more.

The answer involved recovering the main bell wire as we went – a delay we didn't want, especially with the guys using the bell emergency gas.

Everything got rigged up and up came the bell again, albeit slowly. Emergency gas was almost finished and at this point you no longer concentrate on how many hours this has taken, you concentrate on how much time you have left to work with. Unfortunately that was a rapidly diminishing factor.

We'd started to collect the letters of those trapped inside, ready to give to their loved ones.

I remember thinking, 'No more delays please.'

The system mechanic was a little ray of sunshine when he popped into the dive shack and reported he had enough of the main bell winch working again and would like to try it out.

This sounded good but it meant we had to stop doing it the way we were and re-rig in order to allow the main winch to do its job. It would take an hour or so and might not work, but if it did we'd have the boys up and locked on to the main chamber with air, food and warmth in less than 15 minutes. Decision made, the mechanic had been with us a long time and said he was sure it would work.

An hour and a half later, with a very limited depleting gas supply on board, we were ready to give it a go. Thankfully, once the engineer had got the hydraulics of the main bell winch operational again, we were able to get them up to the required depth.

Fifteen minutes later the guys who'd been trapped were in the main chamber with their mates.

The mechanic had been right, as he shared his words of wisdom, 'Next time, he just needs to remember to turn the diesel off.' Little shit.

The boat returned to Peterhead where the divers were decompressed. The boat had some nasty burn marks but everyone had survived. I said my goodbyes to the lads in the chambers before I left with a promise to meet up and have a pint.

Strange, looking at the chambers reminded me of when they were a big part of my life – and that life was only four years ago. When I was in the chamber I never thought about things like this happening, but from the outside looking in it became poignantly apparent just how vulnerable divers are, relying on things like the strength of a seal, the supply of air and the impact of the crew and environment just outside that bell. For a moment I felt grateful for simply being alive.

17

Whoops

BY February 1984 there had been lots of strange happenings in the oil field, and not just the constant name changing in the last three years of the company I was working for, from Wharton Williams Taylor, to Wharton Williams, to 2W. God knows how much this must have cost them on new stationery.

This particular job, I was working in the Red Sea close to the Suez Canal, on board the *Deepwater 1* vessel. It was a big oil field with hundreds of little platforms. The platforms had been there a long time and bits had started to come loose and fall off. We'd won the contract to put things right.

On our deck we had 50 clamps of all shapes and sizes to hold things together for another 20 years, as the existing ones were worn out. The clamps' purpose was to support a riser pipe, which in turn went to a well head, with the final stop being where the oil came out.

Things were going well. We'd just had a container of food delivered, the clamps were flying on, and the sun was shining. We were only a few metres away from where Moses had parted the sea. Mount Sinai was off on the port side and the remains of the Six-Day War were off the starboard side.

I received a call from the deck as they'd just opened the food container. They said that on the front of the first sack of spuds that came out of the container was written, in big black letters,

'A gift to Egypt from the European community.' I was a little shocked and somewhat angry.

I had ordered the food container from an agent on the beach, who was basically selling us food aid that had been intended for starving people in Egypt and Africa. They were so lazy, they couldn't even be bothered to take the food out of the sacks they'd received them in. Made my blood boil. If I'd known any good Samaritans I'd have sent them the photo. From that point on, it always made me suspicious of how much actually gets to the recipients when you donate to charity. There are some disgusting mercenaries out there.

The next morning we finished the task in hand and I asked the captain to move to the next platform.

'What platform?' he said.

'The one over there,' I said, now pointing at nothing. I reckon he thought I'd been out in the sun too long.

'It was there yesterday,' I said. 'Look on the chart.' Sure enough, there should have been a platform. I told him we had four clamps for the now missing platform.

In that part of the world people didn't get too excited about things like missing platforms. About an hour later, we heard from the beach that the platform had been found on the front of a freighter going through the Suez Canal. It had hit it during the night and not even known, or so the captain had said. Sarcastically, I asked the project manager on the beach if the captain wanted the clamps to hold it on. Whatever language he spoke I knew the answer was rude.

This episode almost acted as a prelude to another chapter of my life relating to platforms. The main difference was, the media had a field day with that one.

18

The Death Of
A Platform

ABOUT a year later in January 1985, on a stormy night, a tanker loading platform fell over and broke into two pieces in the Beryl Field, North Sea. The top section including the helipad and loading boom floated away and ended up in Norway. The remaining 278 feet, which included 480 tons of steel lattice work, sank to the sea bed.

It landed on the subsea basalt tanks which were 100 feet long and weighed 220 tons each – multiplied by four. This all landed on the gravity base, some 75 feet square which was filled with ten feet of concrete. Approximately 22,000 tons of the stuff was required to hold the platform in position. This was the deepest demolition job ever attempted by divers in the North Sea. Nothing like a bit of pressure to keep us all sharp.

There were a number of sceptical and concerned parties looking down on us, so it was essential to get the job done and done correctly. With a rumoured 7,500 wreckages out in the North Sea at that point in time, with only knowledge of the whereabouts of around 2,500, many thought this would be another exercise in sweeping things under the carpet. *The New Scientist*, in February 1986, explained:

'Demolishing platforms is a capital expense, so the taxman will have to pay two-thirds of this figure in tax relief. The oil companies would prefer to topple old platforms where they stand or to cut them off 40 metres below the lowest tide level and to dump the rubbish on the spot.

Fishermen, and it is rumoured, submariners want the letter of the law enforced and the sea bed cleared.'

These guys had a point. Fishermen can do without catching their nets on wreckages and submariners can do without becoming a wreck themselves by colliding with an old wreck.

There was also another debate revolving around the usage of disused or abandoned oil platforms. With wreckage sites not being too popular, suggestions of converting them into power stations, casinos or even prisons started to surface. These were conversations well out of my remit, so I focused on the job in hand.

The contract said we would recover every piece that protruded above the natural sea bed. Although we would be using our state-of-the-art vessel with two big heave compensated cranes, February was always a bad month in the North Sea.

We had a plan. Off we set on the *Safe Regalia* to the Beryl Field.

We were going to use high explosives to cut the steel lattice work into small pieces, lift it up and either put it on our deck or dump it on a supply boat for onward shipping.

A high explosive company was contracted to supply shaped charges that wrapped around the steel legs ready to cut them to bits. A load of great big slings and shackles were loaded on board and off we went with enough explosives to start a war.

As with most jobs, we had a lot of meetings with the clients to explain what we were about to attempt. I let the explosives experts do the talking. They had me convinced, albeit they explained their plan at breakneck speed.

All seemed straightforward, but my gut feeling told me it was a bit premature for me to book my helicopter home just yet.

I saw lots of drawings of shaped charges and how they fitted round the steel. The divers tested them on the surface for fitting and it was now time to start and blow stuff up.

'How are they getting on?' I asked the shift supervisor in charge of the dive.

'Great,' he said. 'We've nearly finished putting the first three shaped charges on. In a minute we'll recover the bell and move away ready for the lads to push the plunger.'

I thought I'd go up to the bridge and watch the show.

I'd seen explosives used underwater before but that was only in shallow water and it all seemed a bit undisciplined – nothing like these guys.

Five, four, three, two, one…BANG.

'Fucking hell!' I thought. I was sure we must have blown the bottom of the barge clean off.

The VHF radio on the bridge was blaring away, with a message from a nearby platform (a mile away), shouting at us to stop doing whatever we were doing. Apparently we'd frightened them as well. They had to restrain half of the workers from jumping over the side.

After a few minutes, things calmed down. The boat was still floating with no harm done. The platform manager had been subdued with a promise not to use so many explosives next time and to give them a warning. We decided to go back and see if there was anything actually left.

I thought the idea had been to cut it into manageable pieces and recover bits as we went along, not to blow it up in one go.

'What have we got?' the supervisor asked the diver on the job.

The diver's reply was worrying. He said the first two charges had removed the paint on the first two, but the third piece was still intact. No damage to the steel.

Removing the paint was not our intention. We wanted to blow 350 feet of steel lattice work to pieces. Unfortunately, this went on for ages as the charges simply wouldn't do the business. It turned out that the explosive needed to be flush on the steel, and if there was the slightest gap between the steel and the explosive, you'd be lucky to make a scratch, never mind a dent. It was back to the good old days of underwater burning. This was going to prolong the job immensely.

Over the next month we broke more 100-ton slings, straightened out more 100-ton shackles, and upset many supply boat captains. One poor guy was called in to take a load. It was a great big length of latticed work, just a bit longer than his deck. He called the deck foreman and asked if it would fit his deck. Jimmy replied, he'd measured it and that it'd be a perfect fit. He told him to bring his boat in.

'On my way,' the captain replied. Nearer and nearer he came until he was under the load. A little voice came on the radio.

'Deck foreman, are you sure it will fit?'

'Down on the crane,' said Jimmy.

With a crash it flattened everything on the deck. It was down.

'You see captain, it fitted perfectly.'

When the captain had stopped calling Jimmy names he departed, never to return.

It was a job straight from hell. It took so long to cut the structure up we were forced into lifting bits that were too heavy for the cranes to manage. In the end, after ten tons of high explosives and many warnings from the local platform, the last bit of steel came up.

By this time we had to take out an indemnity for the supply boats as none would come unless we insured them. At one stage our American operations manager had flown out to see what was going on.

I met him and we were on our way to the mess room when we bumped into the unsuspecting boss of the explosives team. The operations manager launched into him saying, 'When I was in the Navy Seals we used to pull the pin out with our teeth, throw the thing, and BANG – nothing left. What are you guys doing? You couldn't blow your nose. You're just a bunch of pussies.'

He said this with such venom the guy was speechless, but that was our man. Maybe he should have brought some of those explosives with the pins in them.

Once all the steel had been recovered it just left the concrete – 22,000 tons of the stuff. Our plan was simple. Get a 20-inch pipe, make one end into a point, fill the remaining 20 feet with concrete, dangle it from the crane just above the concrete, and let it drop from about 20 feet, smashing the concrete to pieces at the bottom of the ocean.

This would then be followed with the biggest grab we could find and recover it to the back of our boat which had a special corral built on the back deck ready to receive mountains of concrete. We found an old coal mining grab they used to use on those big heaps of coal. Perfect. It just needed some modifying to use underwater and we were set to go.

The grab was a monster, taking up half the back deck. I decided when the deck was full and we went into port to unload, we'd leave it on the sea bed. I couldn't wait to get going.

Once on location, the ROV got itself set in position ready to guide the smashing pile up and down. The engineers thought this up and down was going to be the Achilles heel of the 22,000 tons of concrete. Unfortunately, our vessel only had hydraulic cranes, which meant they'd be far too slow when it was time to drop the pointed pipe.

We hired a diesel mobile crane as opposed to hydraulic, and put it on the stern. We used diesel, because it was much faster, which in this case, would give us a good drop speed to smash the thing to bits.

'Down on the crane,' came the order. 'Let it drop.' The crane driver let it go and the pointed pipe filled with concrete landed smack bang in the middle of the heap.

'Up on the crane – let's have a look and see how much has been broken.'

I've got to say it wasn't impressive – two or three lumps at best was all we'd achieved. Up and down, up and down. We tried different Achilles heels to no avail. In the end, our smashing pile disintegrated, the point fell off, and all the concrete came out in a big heap giving us even more to recover. I'd never witnessed so many shaking heads at once.

I decided to give the grab a go to see if this would work.

The ROV guided it into position over the loose stuff with its massive jaws open. The jaws were released and the grab was slowly raised, jaws closing all the time. As it got to the top of the heap they snapped shut, trapping everything inside. Waiting for the visibility to clear, we guessed if the grab was full it would weigh 15 tons or more.

As the visibility cleared the ROV crept closer. It could see the grab moving up and down in the swell. The dust cleared from the enormous grab only to reveal that it hadn't managed to grab one lump of concrete. Zilch, nothing, nada. Several more attempts were made with the same results. It was hopeless. At this point, it had already cost our company about £2m, sadly, without any conclusion. This meant we had already outdone the budget allocated for this job.

We were going to have to rethink the whole thing. Back to the beach with the empty corral, a busted smashing pile, and a massive grab that was going to have to wait until we'd figured a way to break the concrete.

When you get held up at road works, if you're interested in what they're doing, you might see a JCB digger fitted with a spike digging the tarmac up and making a trench. This was just what we needed for our problem.

We found an old digger and converted it from diesel to hydraulic, gave the divers a quick road-digging training session and off we went again full of hope and leaving the lads on the beach to come up with another idea should this fail. Not that it would. You have to be positive in this world.

Over the side with the digger, positioned it on the concrete heap, then got the underwater driver down with his high visibility jacket. Hey, you have to look the part.

It was like a chicken eating corn. Pick, pick, pick, pick – this concrete was tough. Not a dent. The driver couldn't see the tip, he could only feel and hear it going up and down. To make matters worse, if he pushed too hard with the spike he would have turned the digger over and fallen off, making it too dangerous to continue. We put a relief driver on to see if he was any better at it but ended up going back to the beach to see if the lads had come up with a better idea.

It was then that the 'ripper' was born. The ripper consisted of a massive tooth fitted into a frame that would have a heavy duty wire running up to a tugboat which was capable of a 190-ton bollard pull.

The idea was to position the tooth on one side of the concrete heap, the tugboat the other, let out a bunch of wire, get a good angle, then pull the tooth right through the middle of the heap using, we envisaged, 80 to 90 tons of bollard pull – well within its capability.

Tooth day arrived.

The divers positioned it plumb in the middle. They lay the wire right across the top and got the tug to take up the slack, at which point we recovered them to the surface for their safety. We had never done this before. Nobody had.

These ripping teeth were used in quarries for dragging and breaking up solid rock.

Attempt number three got underway.

I'd left the ROV watching the tooth. It was easy enough to see – a great big lump of steel sitting in its frame ready to rip right through just like it would in its normal life as a quarry ripper.

'Okay, captain. Let's put some weight on the wire.'

'Okay,' he replied, 'that's 20 tons.'

'Anything happening?' I asked.

'Nope,' he said.

'Let's put another 20 tons on.'

'Sure thing,' he said.

I asked the ROV operator if he could detect any movement but he couldn't.

'That's 40 tons,' said the captain.

'Anything?'

'Nope,' said the captain.

'Let's have another 20 tons. Bring it up to 60,' I said.

'You've got it,' he said.

The ROV had a great picture of the tooth in its frame sitting behind the concrete.

'That's 60 tons,' said the captain.

'Nothing yet,' I told him. 'Let's have 80 tons.' Surely it'll go in a minute, I thought. Eighty tons is a lot of pull.

Eighty tons comes and goes. We're now going from 100 tons to 120 and getting near to the maximum. The captain of the tug sounded nervous.

There was still no movement down below when suddenly, WHOOSH – the thing took off. The tug reported the weight had come off the wire.

Once the dust had settled the ROV picture showed a gleaming tooth in the same position minus the frame – it'd ripped the tooth clean out of the frame with the frame landing on the other side of the concrete heap.

The tugboat captain reported the new wire which we'd underwritten for £75,000 had parted. Foiled again.

Back to the beach for a new plan.

Next up was a team of quarry blasters who'd flown over from the States. These boys used to blast solid rock using high explosive shaped charges known as 'penguins'. These penguins would be put into cement-filled boxes and placed on top of the concrete heap in a pattern. The force of the explosions would be directed downwards and, in theory, would crumble the concrete into powder which we could then drag about and level out on the ocean floor.

We got busy making the concrete basalt boxes with the penguins ready to lay our first array of 30. Our limit was 30 at any one time. We'd arrived at this number as it was thought to be enough not to upset the neighbours.

It took a while for the first ones as we had to let the concrete in the ballast boxes set. The penguins sat in their boxes looked good to go and ready for their mission to the bottom of the ocean.

We'd changed vessels again and were back on the semi – 'semi' being short for 'semi-submersible barge' meaning it was half-submerged when it was in operational mode.

My first fitness register.

*Getting ready for possibly my first dive –
aged 18.*

*Extensive doctor's note proving my fitness as a
deep sea diver.*

*Air diving in Nigeria. Wearing the Swindell helmet. Note there's a window at the top which allowed
you to look upwards. Nice idea, but not practical as you'd still need to lean back to look up.*

Holding a baby hammerhead shark in Nigeria. One of the smaller creatures I encountered in those waters.

1970 – writing my memoirs 45 years ahead of time.

Dressing my mate Dave for his air dive. Nigeria.

Wishing my mate Alan good luck for his dive. Nigeria.

Wearing all the gear ahead of a dive to make sure it fits and works properly. Nigeria.

Successful with my red snapper fishing in Nigeria.

One of the whirly birds in Nigeria. This was used to take us from Escravos camp to the rig. We'd often come back loaded with fish.

Getting ready to go down into the muddy depths in Nigeria.

George the Welder (wearing the hat).

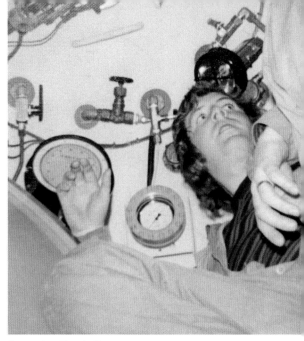

Getting married 1973.

In a saturation bell.

Inside sat control, working for Scan Dive in Norway.

Bottom part is the chamber where you live. Top part is the diving bell which goes on top of the chamber.

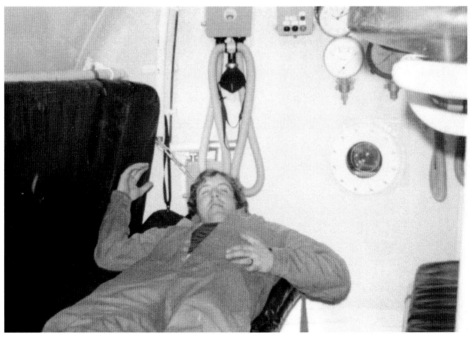

In a decompression chamber after a surface gas jump. I would have been there for about four hours.

Diving bell underwater and welding deep below the ocean surface.

My first saturation job in Norway 1973/4.

On the comms on a diving job.

Handing sandbags to SAS Mike one week before a sat dive. The sandbags were used to stop scouring around the platform legs.

On the Arctic Surveyor *with SAS Mike on the far left. I'm sporting some advertisement for Heinz.*

A bell bounce diving system. The system is now redundant.

Hyperbaric rescue boat.

-20 degrees Celsius in Kristiansand, Norway.

Personnel transfer basket. This is the one which if the waves came over the top, everything got soaked.

Me with a diving bell. Not very big eh?

Part of the base we were trying to blow up on Death of a Platform.

The famous Death of a Platform story – 1986.

Installing a mooring system in Vietnam.

Big chains!

Big anchor!

Deck hands organising the deck in challenging conditions.

A silo going into the ocean in Norway. This would be lowered down and suckered into the seabed using differential pressure.

Standing next to one section of a 107 ton auxiliary flotation tank from the Beryl field mooring.

Remains of a Navy Sea King helicopter we fished out off the coast of Liverpool in 1992.

Listening to what the diver has to say from the bottom of the ocean.

The crane which fell off the barge in Taiwan.

Inside a 65 ton habitat.

Not overly delighted with office life.

Before my illegal dive in Taiwan.

After my illegal dive in Taiwan.

Norfolk man to probe tragedy

NORFOLK engineer David Beckett is to head a diving probe into why the ferry Estonia sank with the loss of 900 lives.

A major condition survey is to be conducted of the Estonia, which could provide vital clues to September's tragedy in the Baltic Sea and give invaluable guidance to other ferry operators.

The operation may also lead to an emotive decision on whether the Estonia will be salvaged from her watery grave.

Mr Beckett, a construction manager from Wrexham, works for the underwater contractor Rockwater. He will be heading for Finland this week to supervise the operation.

"We will be looking at the Estonia with a view to salvage, if that is possible, but it is only an exploratory trip," he said.

"We will carry out an extensive survey to see exactly what's there and also be investigating the cause."

The investigation for the National Maritime Administration in Sweden will be the first in-depth survey and will involve more than 40 divers.

Initial indications of the ferry mishaps her bow door suggested a weakness in the door design. Rockwater will use a semi-submersible diving and construction support vessel, remotely operated vehicles and other equipment in the in-depth survey.

Norfolk engineer leads tragic ferry study team

by DAVID MACAULAY

A diving engineer from Norfolk is to head a diving probe into why the ferry Estonia sank with the loss of 900 lives.

A major condition survey is to be conducted of the Estonia which could provide vital clues to September's tragedy in the Baltic Sea and give invaluable guidance to other ferry operators.

SUMMARY
- Divers plan to examine Estonia in Baltic
- Findings will help other operators

The operation may also lead to an emotive decision on whether the Estonia will be salvaged from her watery grave.

Mr Beckett, a construction manager from Wrexham, works for the underwater contractor Rockwater. He will be heading for Finland this week to supervise the operation.

"We will be looking at the Estonia with a view to salvage, if that is possible, but it is only an exploratory trip," he told the EDP from his Norfolk home.

"We will carry out an extensive survey to see exactly what's there, and also be investigating the cause. We are really just having a good look and relaying back the information."

Mr Beckett has been involved in numerous operations, including the salvage of a Chinook helicopter which crashed in the North Sea, and he is treating the Estonia as another routine job.

"The only thing left to be prepared for finding is bodies."

The investigation for the National Maritime Administration (NMA) in Sweden will see the in-depth survey and will involve no fewer than 44 divers.

Initial pictures of the ferry's bow door suggested a weakness in the door design. Official suggestions the bow of the ferry has now moved on to question the door design of the door. This type of question has now used in UK waters.

Rockwater will use a semi-submersible diving and construction support vessel, remotely operated vehicles and other equipment in the in-depth survey.

The question of salvage, however, remains a controversial one. In sight of the ferry will make memories for families of those who perished in the Baltic. The final decision will be made by NMA.

The ferry Estonia which sank with heavy loss of life

Press re: the Estonia disaster 1994.

The famous deck we had problems putting the cones into the base of Wandoo.

A piece of coal from RMS Titanic. A treasure hunt that unfortunately never happened.

Certificate of Origin

This coal was recovered from the wreck of

R.M.S. TITANIC

during the 1994 Titanic Research and Recovery Expedition

Object No. 94/0036

Authenticated by the signature of

President, RMS Titanic, Inc.   Captain, IFREMER

Down went the penguins.

They were being placed by the divers in a perfect pattern, so that when they were detonated, everything would crumble below.

Ping. Ping.

I asked the diving supervisor what that noise was.

Ping. Ping.

There it was again.

He asked the divers what it was. Nobody knew.

Ping. Ping.

There it was again. Finally, the ROV detected the source of the noise – seems it was the penguins popping out of their ballast boxes, heading for the surface. The cement in the ballast boxes had started to dissolve, setting the little devils free.

I asked, 'What happens if one of these things comes up underneath our vessel and hits the pontoon? Will it go off?' I was getting concerned.

I found it was always good to ask such questions when I was in charge.

'Well, it could,' came the answer I didn't want to hear.

'Could it go off if it hit the platform over there?' I asked.

'Yes it could,' came the answer. Great – the ocean was littered with floating mines.

That's really going to piss them off when I tell them, I thought.

Our captain made speed – we were half a mile away upstream before you could blink. Every window had a set of eyes looking through binoculars trying to spot the penguins. They were heading away from the platform, so I saw no point in frightening them just yet. I didn't want to make history by giving the order for the world's biggest ever full-scale platform evacuation. Not something I fancied on my résumé. We had our rescue boat in the water with one of the Americans on board collecting the penguins as they popped up.

It was late in the day when we got back on location. Thankfully we recovered all the penguins that we'd spotted and the ROV accounted for the rest that were still on the sea bed.

Drama over.

Turns out some nugget had made the concrete used for the ballast boxes with salt water so it never set properly. We later put the penguins in a proper concrete mix which worked – the concrete powdered and we recovered it all. We levelled the rest, took our readings to show the sea bed was once again flat, and departed – £4m poorer.

The job took about a year to complete. With all the events which happened, no wonder *The New Scientist* cashed in and did a six-page scoop.

19

Making History

E VERY cloud has a silver lining, apparently. Despite the debacle with the platform in 1985, the company I was working for at the time (Wharton Williams), known for being one of the best in the industry at hyperbaric welding, did the first pig-less, pup-less and bladder-less weld in the history of the world. This basically cut the process of welding two pipes together in half, so you had just one weld instead of two, not to mention a huge cost saving. The platform site in the Beryl Field provided Wharton Williams with the perfect opportunity to put that weld to use.

What normally happened on a welding job before this weld was implemented, would go something like this: the two pipes to be welded on the sea bed would be roughly aligned and a habitat lowered over them. A couple of handling frames would have been placed a hundred or so feet back up along the pipeline. Everything would have been connected using belly bands – similar to what us humans might wear, but far more robust! A lift on the handling frames and habitat would lift the pipe up inside the habitat. A big rubber seal would be placed around the pipe then fitted to the habitat doors. Once this had been done the habitat would have been filled with the same breathing mix the divers were using. This process would remove all the water from the habitat, leaving the two dry pipes ready to be welded.

We would then put a big rubber bladder inside both pipe ends and inflate them, in order to stop any water in the pipe from coming out when we were welding. Next, both ends of the pipe would be aligned and machined to allow the fitting of the pup piece (a pre-cut piece of pipe). This would be lowered down into the gap between the two pipes. Once in position two welds would be done, with two lots of x-rays required, two lots of non-destructive testing, two lots of ultrasonic testing – two lots of everything plus twice as much risk of something wrong with the welds. Complicated stuff eh?

After the weld had been finished, the pipeline would have to be pigged (a pig is a pipeline cleaner) to remove the bladders, shown in the picture below.

Thanks to further innovative engineering, the handling frames were positioned so they could lift the pipe higher than the weld location in the habitat. This allowed all the water to drain out of the pipes, removing the requirement for the bladders, which in turn meant you didn't need the pig in there to push out the bladder, because there was no bladder anymore! This gave birth to the first ever pig-less, pup-less, bladder-less weld.

At a later date in 1988, there would be an explosion on the Piper Alpha oil rig, which tragically killed 167 people and made global headlines. This disaster created a huge increase hyperbaric welding work at a time when the diving contractors were going through a difficult period. We must have done 30 welds off the back of that explosion, as shut off valves suddenly became very popular.

Our company had some people on that platform when it blew up.

Fortunately, none of them were killed but one of our riggers had his plastic hard hat on at the time of the explosion, and it was so hot it melted on his head and left a very visible permanent scar that was noticeably in the shape of a helmet.

I believe he received a good pay-out and bought a pub in Hull and a Rolls-Royce to get about in, though he couldn't drive so he hired a chauffeur.

20

Missed Opportunities

P RE-PIG-LESS, pup-less, bladder-less weld, I often thought we could have set up the world's largest global drug smuggling operation – or transported something somewhere other than oil!

In many parts of the world, there's a subsea network of pipes from one country to another; from onshore storage tanks to waiting tankers offshore. We welded pipelines together all around the world. Big ones, little ones – you name it, we welded them. The procedure was the same each time.

The pipelines would have been laid by pipe, via lay barges – one from the start country and one from the destination country. Both barges would arrive in the middle and lay the pipe on the sea bed close to each other. Along we came to weld them together. We would have a welding habitat ready to lower over the pipelines so we could pick them up and do a dry weld in a controlled environment. At each end of the pipe, before welding, we'd put two big bladders made of very durable material. You could have filled each bladder full of whatever kind of drugs you liked. Tons of the stuff could have been put into a 36-inch bladder.

Once the weld was finished the bladders would have to be removed. This was done by pushing a pig from one end to the other using water pressure – a lot of water pressure.

A pig had a couple of uses. First, it was fitted with a gauge plate to check the pipes hadn't been bent while being laid. No good having a bent pipeline. Second, they pushed the bladders out of the weld area and down to the end of the pipeline with their valuable cargo.

As for the 36-inch pig that pushed the bladders out, they could have been made into quite luxurious people carriers. As a person on the run, you could have travelled round the pipeline network in comfort. Nobody ever checked them – just the gauge plate to make sure the pipe wasn't bent.

If you were a sinister sort of person you could have fitted it with a bomb. You could even have ten bombs around the globe all at once – it's never-ending. A small pig carrying high explosives and a timer could be pumped from the beach on to a tanker that was loading, then head to a big port in some civilised part of the world. Imagine the damage if it was detonated inside a port, or at the deepest part of the ocean, blowing a pipeline to bits letting tons of oil gush into the ocean killing all the marine life. Although, as history has shown, you don't have to be a terrorist to let a lot of oil spill into the sea.

The merits of the pig got a number of other creative and curious brains working, certainly within the film world, and ended up featuring as a plot device in three James Bond films. James escaped in a pig from a pipeline in *Diamonds Are Forever*, another was used to transport a person into another country in *The Living Daylights*, and the last one was used in *The World Is Not Enough*, where they transported a nuclear weapon through a pipeline.

We saved the world when we introduced pig-less, pup-less welding – perhaps not in a James Bond manner, but we definitely saved the world. Never even got a mention in the New Year's Honours List. Mine must have gone to a football manager for services far more deserving than saving the world.

Although the merits of my efforts in the commercial diving industry in 1985 may have gone unnoticed, on a domestic level I was becoming an aviation pioneer. Albeit, the common theme of blood and disaster had to creep in and spoil everything. Here's what happened.

I'd built a radio-controlled aeroplane which I used to fly around the garden. For no particular reason, I decided to turn it into a sea plane, as back at that time I had a swimming pool in the garden. While it was sitting on the ground with the nylon propeller still whirling around, I saw my son going to grab it and instead I jumped in front of him and picked it up myself. The thing nearly cut my finger off. I ended up at the hospital with several stitches and a number of follow-up operations to get the hand and fingers back in working order again. Unfortunately one of my fingers never fully bent after that occasion, but I was lucky to not lose the feeling in all the fingers and my hand, as most of the tendons had been near-on severed. If you are wondering about the fate of the plane – it came to an abrupt end a short while after, as it ploughed straight into one of my hedges.

Who would have ever thought, at that point of my life, after all the years of near-death experiences around water, that the worst injury I suffered would be on land at the hands of a radio controlled aeroplane? I guess I was at my most confident at home and possibly my most reckless, whereas I never took the power of the ocean for granted, not even for one second and always abided by the rules below the surface.

Or perhaps technology wasn't my thing. It certainly didn't do my family any credits a few years later.

21

Rumbled

'A dive superintendent (described as "an oil worker" despite his yacht, his Mercedes and his £350,000 house) was fined £5,000.'

(*Private Eye* – Edition 773, 2 August 1991)

THE early 1990s started off in blistering fashion. Well, the burns almost caused a few. My brother was friends with another diver who had helped to invent a gizmo which could turn back the dials on your electricity meter. It was a touch of genius in all honesty – although honesty is perhaps not the best word for this particular anecdote.

They had one of these devices plugged into their own electric meter and suspicion arose when the electricity board quickly clocked on that the current reading was less than the previous one.

My brother had asked if I wanted one fitted and I agreed, not seeing any major harm. When turning it on, the thing blew up and scorched the surrounding wall area. I decided at that moment that we would give it a miss.

However, when the electricity board came to check my meter, they saw the scorch marks around it and quickly worked out that

I must have been operating a similar device to my brother. They then cut the meter out and took it away for examination to see if it had been tampered with. They quickly realised it had. It cost me a grand to get a new meter fitted immediately. So much for saving money!

Having been rumbled, we all ended up in court. My brother was sentenced to a year in prison, of which he served three months. While feeling bad for him, I was ready to stand up and get on with my day, when the judge addressed me and said, 'David Beckett – we are going to sentence you to two months in prison.' My heart dropped – seriously dropped. There was a pause before she continued her sentence and continued, 'Which will be suspended, and you will also pay a £5,000 fine.' I couldn't believe it. I've never panicked or been scared during all my diving career, but I reckon I was more shaken hearing that I might go to jail, than I'd ever been in my life. The judge was trying to put the frighteners on me and she'd succeeded – with gusto.

Our names ended up in the papers and a feature was written up in *Private Eye* entitled 'On The Rigs'. It was nowhere near as funny as *On The Buses*.

My daughter was at school a few days later and one of her friends asked her while holding a copy of a local newspaper, 'Is your dad's name David Beckett?' She swiftly replied with a smile on her face, 'No,' and changed the subject rather quickly.

Although the article which *Private Eye* covered was a very unfortunate episode, it was correct in that I did have a yacht at the time called *The Swageroo,* or our pet name for it was 'a shag or two', can't think why. It was a wooden-built trawler yacht capable of crossing any sea and had done the Bay of Biscay a couple of times.

Despite the yacht having been picked up in the media as an indication of fortune, the vessel turned out to be more of a misfortune/jinx.

The first challenge I had when picking it up from Ipswich was getting it back to Great Yarmouth. After the captain gave me the once over on how you worked the sat nav, I figured, as a technophobe, that I could use it to get me back to Great Yarmouth. I did however bring my gigantic Esso road map as back-up. Halfway through the voyage the sat nav said that I was going down the high street in Bury St Edmunds! Even I knew that was wrong.

Having got this 45-foot beast home, I now envisaged good times ahead – although, as a non-domestic god at that time, I never imageded how testing the cleaning side of things would become.

Wooden boats have been about for ages and so have our feathered friends. Elderberries grow in abundance by the river – they produce a lovely purple berry and birds just love them. I think that they had a laxative effect on them though, as the birds would sit on the boat and poo a lovely purple colour that stained the paint, which as yachts should be, was white. The old *Swag* was swiftly becoming purple, so much so that I used to spend a considerable amount of my time painting the bloody thing.

Whenever I was doing maintenance on it, my kids would come for the ride, would do a bit of fishing from the deck, feed the ducks and do what kids do best – fool about.

On one occasion, my son Guy was fishing from the top deck with his life jacket on, golden rule they must wear their life jackets at all times, when suddenly I saw him go past the cabin window with his fishing rod in hand. I remember thinking, that's a big one. A passing boat pulled him out for me – no harm done – lesson learned, stay the right side of the handrails. Shortly after, my daughter did the same thing. She was on the bathing platform feeding the ducks, when she reached over and kept going! Luckily I made them clip a safety line on to their life jacket after my son's episode, so she didn't stray that far.

Not content with falling overboard, my son decided to raise the bar. The old *Swag* had a little boat on the top deck called a Stingray – a small speedboat-type craft with a 10hp engine, which was controlled by a joystick and on full plane was quite fast.

On the river there is a 5mph speed limit, so whenever Guy used it I told him no more than 5mph. On this particular day, he was out of sight and round the bend in the river, when I heard the river police boat's siren flash up. Next thing, Guy came flying round the corner with the police boat in hot pursuit. At this point they were both doing over the speed limit. I paid the fine. Boys will be boys.

Nobody was immune to the jinx of the *Swag*. One day I thought that we would have a big adventure and go offshore.

Not far from the entrance to the river at Great Yarmouth is a sand bank called Scroby Sands. It's infested with seals and I thought it would be nice to get up close for our kids and their friends to see them. Afterwards we could drop anchor, they could fish and I could cook them some lunch. With my provision steak and kidney pie (the ones you heat in the tin with mashed potatoes, peas, and a bit of gravy), I was fully prepped.

I was just about to hit the dinner gong when the wife screamed. Up on deck she was holding her hand with a big fish hook stuck in her thumb. One of the kids had got in a tangle and she was helping untangle the mess when he dropped the fishing weight for some reason and the weight pulled the hook into her thumb. Trouble was, it didn't go right through, so it was stuck in there and I couldn't cut the end off and pull it out.

Lunch was a disaster, everyone was seasick and couldn't eat, and the wife was in agony.

Back to Great Yarmouth we went to find a doctor. We found Dr Death on the quay who I thought my wife was going to plant with a right hand when he tried to pull the hook out. In the end we went to the local hospital to have it removed properly.

We sold the *Swag* shortly afterwards. So much for the dream holidays.

22

More Helicopters

DESPITE having seen my fair share of helicopter disasters, they are still a far faster and cleaner way to change crew than the old system.

In the old days, we used to change crew using a supply boat, as the barges simply didn't have helidecks. Most of the early barges used in the North Sea had been towed over from the States – usually with the good old boys still inside playing poker. I don't think anyone of them knew where they were going. The good old boys liked things to be just like home, but they soon found out things were slightly different in the North Sea.

A typical crew change out of Great Yarmouth would start in a pub. The guys would wait in the pub until the boat had been fully loaded with its cargo and was ready to sail. There would normally be between 12 and 14 guys changing crew. That's all the supply boats were allowed to carry. It had something to do with how many places they had in the lifeboat.

When it was time to leave, you got the call to board and those that could still walk, made their way to the boat. It was 20-odd hours' steam to the barge from Great Yarmouth to the North Sea, so you got time to sleep it off. Everyone was in the same cabin which made it nice and cosy, especially after 12 men fully fuelled on local beer started to digest dinner.

The first time I did this trip as a rookie diver, I went straight for a bottom bunk, simply because it was not so far to fall if it was rough and a lot more convenient for the loo. When I got the bunk, I thought, 'That was easy!' It wasn't until the first person was sick that I realised why the old boys went straight for the top bunks. Next thing, the engines started, the boat shuddered and we started to move away from the quay. I lied back on my brown-stained mattress, minus a bed sheet, as we started our next adventure.

Out of the breakwater we went. The engines were opened up and the boat came to life as it started hitting the waves. Then, it turned sideways and began to roll as the sea came from the side, giving it a nasty motion. It's at this point your feel like you are in a cocktail mixer, with about 40 pints of beer sloshing about the cabin floor and a welder in the bunk above not caring if his went all over me or not.

The journey was a nightmare. You could get a cup of coffee if the cook liked you but, as he would explain, it would always be out of the goodness of his heart. 'We don't get paid to feed or water you, just transport you.'

When the journey was over and we arrived at the barge, it was a relief when they told us to get out on deck ready to be lifted by the barge's crane. We took our bags and headed for the personnel basket. If it was wet on the deck timing was everything – unless you fancied a bagful of salt water. Although, your feet nearly always got wet.

The personnel basket held four people. The procedure involved slinging the bags in the middle of the basket, taking the life jackets that were inside, putting them on, then clinging to the outside of the basket while getting snatched from the heaving deck. If the crane driver was good, it went well. If he was bad, anything could happen, including getting severely soaked, the basket sliding across the deck and smashing into the bulkhead, or your bags falling out. You could probably say the basket-sliding scenario was the most severe.

Once up in the air, the relief was fantastic. You could see your bag with the water dribbling out but you didn't care, as you were off the deck of the supply boat.

You'd land on the barge and jump out, grab your bag, put your life jacket back in the basket and get as far away from it as possible, before it took off ready for the next lot of people. You didn't even care when you realised the life jacket was covered in grease and your going-home shirt had just been ruined.

Going back was even worse. I used to stay up and sit in the galley. I took my own food and coffee from the barge. The barges, in those days, sold duty free cigarettes and cigars. I used to fill a black poly bag with some of each and the wife would wait at the harbour entrance, then follow the boat upriver. At the nearest point where the boat came to the quay, I'd throw the bag of goodies over the wall and she'd go and get it. No sir, nothing to declare. Bottom line – give me a helicopter any day.

The Chinook crash I worked on in 1986 made history for all the wrong reasons – simply because it was one of the biggest helicopter disasters of all time. It came laden with horrific scenes, many of which made a number of people change careers. The only tiny redeeming factor, from a selfish perspective, which helped soften the blow was that I didn't have to witness the crash itself or see anyone die close up. Unfortunately in 1991, in the Ekofisk oil field, I wasn't spared that luxury – albeit, believe it or not, a crashing helicopter was the least of my worries.

The task in hand on this occasion was hyperbaric welding and construction work.

Down we went and landed on the helideck of the *Semi 2* vessel. It was a big crew change – off with the old welding crew and on with the new. For some reason they never stopped the rotor blades from whooshing round, so everything was done in the head-down position. You picked up your bags and walked like an ape to the stairs. Only then did you feel safe and that you wouldn't be decapitated. The off-going crew were gathered at the bottom of the stairs, grim-faced. They smiled when they saw us. Once they saw you, touched you, they knew they were on their way home.

Once we were inside, the lads had to wait to find their cabin number. Not me, I knew mine – it was the biggest one. I slung my bags in the cabin and headed for the bridge as per my usual routine. All the people I needed to talk to would be there – my dive superintendent who knew what was going on; the captain who was determined to break your hand with his handshake; and the dear old company rep who wanted to know if you'd brought any fresh porn.

The vessel had to pull away from the platform to let the helicopter land. As soon as it left we moved back in, launched the bell, and continued work. The dive superintendent had everything under control. All the equipment for the welding job was on board and the welding superintendent knew what to do, so that could mean only one thing for me – lunchtime.

The mess room was always a good place to be reacquainted with the lads. They did 12-hour shifts – midday until midnight, so you saw the oncoming shift and the off-going shift. You had to eat a lot to see them all, but the food was good. I normally started at six in the morning and got to bed once the midnight shift had started – four meals a day or 18 hours. I tried not to eat between meals.

Meetings, people love meetings. Sometimes the meetings were about meetings, or for the sake of having a meeting to tick the corporate strategic box. We had one a day – a progress meeting, every morning at ten o'clock. The first one on a new job was always a big one, because the client was trying to find out if you had read the procedures. I always let the engineer do the first one just to prove we had, as he was usually the only one who had. After all, he wrote them. After that, my lot didn't say a word unless I asked them something.

I learnt long ago, that the more people who spoke, the more things could get confused. I figured we were here to weld a pipe together safely and within a scheduled time. That was my job, so I did the talking.

There was quite a lot of concern about welding on a pipeline full of gas using our new gasproof pig with an isotope. The procedures said it had passed all the safety checks, but we were going to monitor the atmosphere continually once the habitat was in position. The first test involved finding the pig with the diver handheld pig locator.

We had a couple of days' prep work before the habitat went down, so things were busy. Since we were so close to a live gas platform we worked to a very strict work permit system. The permits were withdrawn and re-issued every 12 hours. This was done between the boss of the platform and the bridge crew on the semi.

There was absolutely no smoking on the deck and if you wanted to do any welding or burning on the deck, you needed a hot work permit. A 'hot work permit' is not a hookie one, it's literally what is says on the tin, in so much as it's anything live heat related. At that point the others working on the vessel would have to ensure thing likes gas were not in operation, or anything that didn't react well with flames.

If Jack the lad decided to have a fag on the deck he would have most probably set off all the water cannons pointing our way. It would have most certainly put his fag out. It was in the interests of both parties that there were no flames and no gas.

Nothing much had happened the first night. The divers were just knocking concrete off the subsea pipe in the area. The pig was being prepared for us, so we could cut the old bit out. On the platform they were getting ready to put the pig with the diver-friendly isotope down the pipe.

The habitat was being prepared ready for launch. I had my first coffee of the day on the bridge while talking to the dive superintendent and the captain. Things were just great, so it was time for the first meal of the day – a slap-up breakfast.

It might just be me, but being the boss and walking into the mess room and seeing all the lads gave me a bit of a buzz. They were all pleased to see me and there was always lots of banter. It was a great feeling, though I have had the odd hiccup along the way and I think it's fair to say that I had picked up a bit of a reputation.

Some people, when they first meet, can be a bit wary of you. After all, we did have the power to hire and fire. And when I say this can happen in a New York second, I mean it can happen in a New York second. One moment you're on £100k+ a year; next minute you're on the helicopter back to the beach. Things might have changed a bit nowadays but it was a good system which kept everyone sharp.

I remember, one day, walking into the mess room on to a new barge with an inherited crew, and you could have heard a pin drop. I imagined they were saying, 'Here comes big head. What's so good about him?'

I got my meal from the counter, picked up my favourite sauce bottle and made my way to an empty table. I was doing my best to act ultra cool. I gave the bottle a good shake when the fucking lid came off. The sauce went everywhere; ceiling, floor, down my shirt. Heads went down to hide their reactions, but I could see their shoulders bouncing up and down with laughter.

Next morning proved just what work permits were all about. That piece of paper should have ensured that platform was intrinsically safe, with no gas discharge of any kind whatsoever. My morning call informed me, during the night when they were loading the pig into the pipe, they'd managed to release enough gas across our deck to send us into orbit, should someone have been sitting there with a burning torch. Had it exploded there would have been a paper trail all the way to Mars. Thank goodness for the validity of permits eh?

They'd managed to overcome the problem and the pig was making its way down the pipe to the cut location. It was almost time to set the diver free with the pig locator.

The first big test.

Around midday, the pig was in position, so we sent the diver down to see what we could find. Pretty soon we detected a signal. Not a very good signal, but nonetheless, a signal. Only problem was, they'd overshot the cut location with the pig. With a little bit of messing, we got it into the right position ready to inflate. Once inflated, they filled the pipe with water and we were ready to cut it. The first cut was always nerve-wracking, as there might have been a gas pocket – a little tester for the diver's ears and nerves.

With all the upfront subsea work finished, 12 hours later we were ready to launch the habitat. The pig was doing its job, there were no gas bubbles coming out and the habitat checks were complete. It looked like we were on to a winner.

This thing weighed 65 tons so it had to be nice and calm when we sent it overboard. Up she went, over the side.

Inside the habitat, there was a line which we watched. It was essential that the water did not come above it as things inside would get wet. As the habitat went down, people in the welding shack watched the line and the water. When the water got near the line they opened the gas line to the habitat and blew gas into the habitat, keeping the water just below the line. It's like turning a glass upside down in the kitchen sink and the air stays trapped. If you bring the rim off horizontal, water comes in. Same with this, except, the air the crew were blowing in, helped to maintain a safe environment if a tilt did happen.

At least, that's what should have happened.

On top of the habitat was an emergency hatch, just in case we had to rescue the divers. However, some idiot had forgotten to put the rubber seal in, and as the gas was pissing out bubbles everywhere we had no option but to recover it to the deck and put the seal in.

The lads on the deck were trying to get the habitat back on board, but they were having difficulties in getting the crane driver to hear what they were saying because of the racket from a helicopter directly above us, which was attempting to lower a piece of pipe on top of a flare stack.

Then suddenly – BANG. Disaster struck.

There was a hell of a crashing noise, swiftly followed by pieces of helicopter dropping out of the sky and more worryingly, followed by bodies.

The pipe the helicopter was carrying had hit the top of the stack and tilted up until it hit the tail rotor, sending the helicopter out of control. The co-pilot was thrown out of the door and sent crashing into the water beside our vessel. He was just about alive at this point, but we were unable to get our boat into the water quick enough to save him or rescue his body. The captain ended up on some bracings just above us, upper body facing one way and feet the other, and the third man hit the walkway at such speed his body was flattened and surrounded by a massive pool of blood.

The captain immediately started running up and down in a right state. I guess he thought the helicopter might land on his deck and sink us. Thankfully it never did. It had missed and what hadn't disintegrated on the way down fell into the sea. Lucky escape for us, but not those in the helicopter.

Despite the fact that a helicopter was literally sinking in front of our eyes and people had just died, our immediate priority was to recover the habitat. Having a 65-ton weight swinging over the front of the boat was enough to cause a major disaster.

Thankfully, by about midnight, the habitat was down and in position. The lads had more than 12 hours to get things sorted before we started welding. I went to dinner just after midnight with little appetite, keeping my fingers crossed that something could start to go right.

What a day.

I often wondered what would have happened if the helicopter had crashed on to our deck making it impossible for us to recover the divers. Thankfully I didn't have to deal with that scenario. Besides, this one was bad enough.

23

Fun In The Jungle

NOT long after leaving the Ekofisk field, I was informed that I'd be working in Brunei on yet another hyperbaric welding job.

After landing at Bandar Seri Begawan airport, I headed to the heliport to fly to my final stop.

Turns out we would be flying in a Chinook. I started thinking, 'I hope they've found a solution to the gearbox problem.' I didn't fancy getting hauled up in a cargo net with seagulls pecking at me. It's not exactly the end I had in mind.

Whenever you flew anywhere in a helicopter, you had to pop a survival suit on and watch a video that showed you how to get out of a helicopter should it crash into the sea. Always great to get the spirits up, especially for those with a fear of flying.

If you've never had to put a survival suit on, you're lucky. It's a bit like getting into a diving suit until you pull the rubber neck seal over your head. Some of the lads had to take out their earrings.

The rubber neck ring is, as you can probably imagine, very tight. It has to make a seal around your neck, so the 'going over your head' part is nasty. The wrists are the same but not as bad as the head seal.

I guess your hands are not as big as your head and your hands don't have as much hair as some of us. This could be where the bald guys benefited.

Once the suits were on, out we would waddle to the waiting chopper and got strapped in ready for take-off. Some guy would have a quick look to see if we were strapped in, then he was off with a slam of the door before starting the engines and lifting off.

However, before you got this far you had to go through an offshore survival course which entailed sitting in a helicopter in a swimming pool.

The survival course only lasted four years and mine had run out. As I was doing this job in Brunei, my client Shell told me to attend a course locally, to save time and money, which made logistical sense. The jungle of Borneo it was!

During my first day I never understood a word the guys said as they harped on in Malaysian, but I figured someone at Shell thought it was doing me good.

Next day was helicopter rollover day.

The instructor informed us they were going to turn the whole thing upside down, at which point we would have to release our belt and make an exit through the window nearest to us. Oh, and don't forget to take a deep breath. Over you went, undid the belt and out you came. Simple.

They had a big pool and a full-sized helicopter. The local guys had their best swimsuits on and although they didn't speak English, the instructor was showing them the belt and the window. I figured he was giving them the lowdown on what to do. Finally, he indicated that we all get in. Being a gentleman I let them get in first. We British are famous for our manners.

In they all clambered. Then in I got. That's lucky, I thought, I'm right next to the door. It's a lot easier to get out of the door.

The instructor gave us the hand on the strap routine, showed us the window and me the door, then gave us the thumbs-up. The local guys all put their thumbs up and smiled at him. Out he jumped and they switched a wave machine on. There's a first time for everything. I'd never done the drill in the waves before, but why not. After all, should I crash, there'd be a good chance the sea would be rough.

The instructor blew his whistle to let us know we were just about to be turned upside down. It seemed to take quite a while to turn over, but over we went. I took a deep breath, waited until we stopped, then released my strap and out the door I went. I popped up in the choppy pool, with the whole exercise taking no more than ten seconds.

There I was now, going up and down in the pool waiting for the locals to pop up.

I reckon a full minute must have passed before the guys operating the helicopter started shouting at each other, giving the signal to lift it up out of the water. Up it came, upside down, with all the locals still strapped in. Not a good day for them.

They turned the helicopter upright again and the instructor gave them what must have been a bollocking, because they all nodded and put their hands back on the seat belts before giving the thumbs-up sign which meant they were ready for another go.

The instructor indicated for me to get back in as we were going to do it again. You would have thought they'd have let me off doing it again – after all, I'd already survived once.

The whistle went again, over we went and as before, up I popped. But, once again, there was no sign of the locals. By this time I'd had enough, so I got out of the pool and watched them bring the helicopter up again, full of the upside down men.

God knows why they couldn't do it properly.

I got my certificate at the same time as they got theirs. Just because you can't do it properly doesn't mean you don't get a certificate, not in the jungle anyway.

When I watched safety videos from that point forth, I used to look around the room thinking to myself, 'I wonder where they've sat their course – hopefully not Borneo.'

24

Another Plough Bites The Dust

A FAIR bit was crammed in to 1992. Everything from recovering a Navy Sea King helicopter off the coast of Liverpool, which was on the sea bed 200 feet below the surface, through to a number of construction jobs throughout the globe. One of which would eventually force me to get my old diving gear on again.

The Singapore office had a bad job going in Taiwan. It was well over schedule with no end in sight. I told them thanks, but I really didn't want to go as I knew it would be a real pain.

Despite my best attempts to get out of it, the bottom line was, 'Make sure your passport is valid David – you leave tomorrow morning.'

Several hours after leaving Heathrow, looking out the window of the 747, we just about cleared the washing lines on top of the skyscrapers coming into Hong Kong airport. Just as I started to remind myself how safe air travel was, the pilot seemed to lose control of the thing and banked to the right, big time. I figured we'd just missed a skyscraper or something when, suddenly, he got it level just in time to land on a runway that went out to sea. Apparently, this was a regular landing style. A heads-up would have been nice.

Next up was a quick flight on China Airways, with the destination being Kaohsiung in Taiwan. The flight was too short for a hot meal so the choice was a tin of some kind of beans or another tin of something I didn't catch the name of. I had the beans. You can't go wrong with beans – well, not until you took the lid off. Stink? I've never smelt anything like it, and trust me, I've been exposed to some rancid smells.

'You no like your beans?' the stewardess asked.

'I think they're off,' I said. 'Could I have a drink instead, please, with a biscuit?' She gave me a disgruntled look and handed over what I asked for as if I'd asked her to hand over her family fortune.

After landing, thankfully a little smoother than the Hong Kong scene, I headed to the carousel to pick up my luggage. It's not a good sign when you're the last one waiting. It normally means – and this was no exception – that they've lost your bags. Great. Off I trotted to the compensation desk, where they gave me $200 to tide me over, until they found my bag – if they found my bag.

I told the agent, who met me at the airport, we were going shopping before we went to the hotel, and asked whether he knew of any good clothing shops. What a silly question in Taiwan. You could get any of the major brands. They even looked real. Little did I know that replacing an entire wardrobe only cost $100 and even better, a few days later my bag also re-appeared.

The town centre was an eye opener. It was strange seeing five people on one Lambretta, but the agent told me this was quite normal and that he'd seen more than five on one bike – his bike in fact.

The pollution was so bad they all wore these little white face masks. I remember thinking that look wouldn't go down too well in Trafalgar Square.

I was dropped off at the hotel with my new wardrobe and was ready to meet the project manager for dinner and a briefing.

The guy's name was Henk, a Dutchman. We'd met a few times before in Singapore over the last five years. He was a nice chap but at his wits' end with this job. Sounded a bit of a nightmare just dealing with the people. He told me he'd organised my transport for the next morning at 5.30am, which would take me to a boat, and in turn that boat would run me out to the offshore barge.

Sure enough, at 5.30am the driver turned up and off we went.

I loved the 'no speak English' routines. The driver pointed at some rocks where all I could see was a big canoe with an engine hanging off the end of a long stick, and a large, fat, bald Taiwanese man looking straight at me. It was foggy and there was no sign of any barge on the horizon. It was times like these when I began to wonder if I was doing the right thing.

The Taiwanese guy couldn't speak English and my Taiwanese was non-existent. I couldn't see the barge and I was trying to avoid customs. No wonder this job has gone bad, I thought.

Henk had given me a telephone and enough sim cards to last me a fortnight. He had told me to change the card every day as the locals cloned them. I thought about ringing him and asking for a bigger boat, then I remembered that I was Dave the diver and got in the canoe. Off we went out, into the hazy mist, me and the Taiwanese guy.

Lo and behold, out of the haze appeared the barge. It was an old barge but it was now my refuge and was also going to be home for longer than I expected or would have wanted.

When I walked on to a job that was not going very well, it came as no surprise when they hit me with the 'we don't need you' attitude. You might not need me I thought, but I'm here to stay and finish the job that you're fucking up. Well, that was my attitude anyway and I quickly needed to let them know that or I may as well have gone home.

I never liked the superintendent, so it was no problem getting rid of him. His engineer had a very hairy neck and I didn't like that, so he had to go as well.

Before I'd left the UK I insisted my own superintendent and engineer would soon follow behind me. With the two new vacancies suddenly appearing, I'm quite glad I'd insisted. It was nice to have good company when I was miles from home, especially when I was surrounded by morons who thought I was an overpaid prick.

Having to make some harsh decisions early on, I soon realised it paid to lock my cabin door at night. I didn't want to wake up in the morning, floating around in the South China Sea with a weight around my neck. I'm not kidding.

Even the oil company reps had attitude, largely because our people had allowed them too much input on the job and they felt like they were in charge.

The job was straightforward. Install an oil tanker loading buoy and bury the pipeline a metre deep all the way to the beach. Problem one was, we hadn't finished installing the buoy – problem two was we couldn't bury the pipeline. Fundamentally – not great.

The sea bed was so hard, the underwater plough wouldn't penetrate it. As an ex-farmer boy I know the size of a plough and I can tell you, these ploughs were massive. The main issue that occurred with these ploughs happened if the angles of the blades were symmetrically wrong. It was like trying to pull a huge brick along – it was never going to happen.

In the North Sea we used big sledges fitted with high pressure water jets.

These were lowered over the pipe and the jets would then be fired up, as we blasted a big trench while dragging the sledge along. It was looking likely that this would be our way forward.

The installation of the buoy was very slow. The divers were having trouble with the poor-to-nil visibility and were taking an age to get anything done. The whole barge was having trouble in my opinion.

I was sat in the office when, to my surprise, I saw the mobile crane disappear past the window followed by a loud bang. It had just fallen over the side and it landed on a supply boat that was tied up alongside.

The driver had gotten too close to the side of the barge and together with the swell, as he boomed down to lift his load from the supply boat, the barge started to rock…and rock.

The driver had had enough sense to jump out of the cab before the last rock. Moments later, the crane went over the side, landing on the supply boat so hard it nearly turned it over. Suffice to say, there were a lot of alarms going off at the same time.

Finally, Harry and my engineer Richard arrived via the same mode of transport – a Taiwanese guy and a canoe. With a sarcastic tone I greeted them, 'You pair are going to love it on here! Just to let you know, we ran out of food two days ago. It's sandwiches or nothing.' I could tell they were very excited to be here.

With no mobile crane to lift food containers on board, we were dependent on the big rig to lift things for us in the swell. They were being very careful with the big rig.

I'd made my mind up that the barge was not suitable for this job. The office agreed. All that was left was for me to tell the company rep that we were demobilising the barge and would remobilise another vessel.

'You can't do that,' he said.

'See that canoe with the Taiwanese guy? Well, it's coming to pick me and my men up and take us to the beach. See you in two weeks when we come back with our own vessel.' That was the end of that.

25

Typhoon

TWO weeks wasn't long, but in that time we'd chopped up a jetting sledge in the UK, loaded it on a 747, and had it delivered to Taiwan where we would reassemble it fit for purpose.

The DP boat had arrived from Singapore and was being loaded. We had our own company divers this time round, so I was much more confident than before. Even the company rep agreed it might have been for the best.

The jet sledge came complete with its own good old boy from the swamps and a couple of Spanish riggers. I listened to the good old boy explaining to the rep how it worked. He was going on about the angle of the jets and how many you should have; how you had to have just the right amount of water pressure; then, lastly, how the speed that pulled the sled was critical to the performance of his jet sledge. By the time he'd finished explaining things to the rep, they'd both bought into his bullshit and I think they both believed it would work.

Back on site, I figured we might as well get on with burying the pipe first, since we were rigged and ready. The Spanish lads lowered the two big suction pipes over the side and welded them into position ready to suck up the vast amount of water required for the jetting sledge.

Before we lowered the sled over the pipe, we gave it a test on the deck – slowly at first, to check all the jets were working.

Then we opened the pump right up and the sled nearly took off. I didn't know which way his nozzles were pointing but there was more spray than when you overtake an articulated lorry on the M1 during a cloudburst – you couldn't see a thing.

We were ready to put it over the pipe and get jetting. The divers were waiting on the sea bed ready to guide the sled into position. As usual the visibility was crap and they heard it bounce on the pipe before they found it. There was loads of concrete on these pipes so it did no harm.

The guys got it over the pipe and moved away a little, ready to fire the pumps up. We did a few metres then checked the trench depth.

Everything was roaring away on deck. You could see something was happening. Down below, the water was bubbling away on the surface and we were moving forward at a nice, steady pace.

From memory I think they wanted about half a metre burial from the top of the pipe to the sea bed. The divers reported that it was working fine. The good old boy must have had his jets pointing in the right direction. At the speed we were going I figured we'd be done with the trenching in a week, which was good news for the lads on the beach.

However, in the meantime, captain George had some bad news for me. There was a typhoon forecast in the next couple of days in our area. Despite the North Sea being pretty shitty on occasions, I'd never been in a typhoon before. The nearest I got was on a boat in the Norwegian sector and we had waves not far off 90 feet for three days. Just to put this into perspective, the structures that are built in the sea take into consideration the hundred year wave and as a result, the walkways are 100 feet above the surface of the sea.

Now imagine being in a boat in the middle of the ocean. You felt about four times your weight as the ship rose up the wave, but weightless that moment before it dropped. Kind of like a rollercoaster, or that feeling when driving over a humpback bridge at great speed. One second you would see sky and the next, bang, you had hit the water again and saw nothing but water until the next surge upwards.

The only difference was, if the wave was big and bad enough, you wouldn't live to tell the tale of the adrenaline rush to future generations. That storm in Norway sent us nuts as we couldn't sleep. As much as we tried to jam the items of our cabin against or under something, it was a losing battle. Taking a shower was a nightmare and sitting on the loo was like riding a bronco.

You were basically in the hands of the competence of the captain and the build of the boat. Many captains would have turned around, but not ours. When it calmed down a bit they noticed one of the lifeboats had been washed away from the port side. Not that it really mattered as no one would have got in it anyway.

Back to the pending typhoon in Taiwan, captain George explained to me, 'When the typhoon approaches, the air will turn green, then, a couple of hours later all hell will break loose, so make sure you're ready.'

Captain George was Indian, so he knew a thing or two about typhoons.

'Thanks,' I said. 'Just give me the nod and I'll make sure things are fast on the deck.'

Most things were welded down before we left the safety of the harbour and checked by the insurance company. It was only the little things you had to take care of, such as shackles, steel oil drums and basically anything that could fly about and do damage.

When the call came that the air was turning green, I gave the order to disconnect all the hoses from the sledge, tie down anything that had the potential to fly off and make everything fast.

Unless you've experienced a typhoon yourself, it's hard to describe. The air was still and there was a green haze – not like fog, just a haze. It was nothing like the light show that comes with the Northern Lights. The green air was almost like a warning, similar to when the ocean goes out just before a tsunami is about to hit. This was literally the lull before the storm.

We were ready.

Within the hour, the rain came lashing down, but as opposed to the ship in Norway that time, this time we couldn't see out of the windscreen. Then the wind picked up. Great! At this point captain George was heading straight into the storm, totally relying on the deck instruments, which weren't working efficiently due to the weather. Risky stuff.

Although nobody was panicking, people were throwing up all over the place. Many tried all sorts of things such as putting patches behind their ears, taking tablets and even a few swigs of alcohol, but none of it worked in those conditions. Luckily I never got seasick.

Captain George decided we should high tail it to the harbour for safety. We'd just heard a mayday from a boat that'd been washed up on the beach. It was only about half an hour's steam, so captain George set off in the general direction using his radar in an attempt to assist.

The radar screen was clustered with the rain, making it virtually useless, but captain George was on his way to the safety of the harbour. Just as we neared the mouth of the harbour, the lights turned red and the harbour master came on the radio turning all boats away saying it was too dangerous to come in.

We had no option but to turn away and find a place to ride the storm.

A few minutes later, captain George's eyes went almost white as they were opened so wide. We'd just missed another boat that was trying to get into the harbour.

I asked him how long this was likely to last. 'Twenty-four hours,' he replied. I'd better go and find a life jacket, I thought.

The typhoon was probably the worst storm I'd ever experienced, but by the end of the 24 hours, we could see out of the windows of the bridge again – though what we saw was not good. My big suction pipes had been washed away. Dammit – just when things were going well and with only a little left to do.

I decided I wouldn't make a drama out of it. I'd just connect back up to the sledge, fire up the pumps, make lots of noise on deck so things looked normal, and drag the sled to the end of the pipe. Job done.

Once we'd got rid of the sled and all the merry men that came with it, it was time to finish installing the buoy. There wasn't too much to do, but the job was going slowly as the divers were struggling with the black water and I too was getting frustrated.

I got so pissed off one day that I decided to go and have a look for myself. On the buoy was a standby air dive station. I asked one of the riggers to give me his overalls and man the air dive radio, sling a load of slack hose over the side, and put his foot on it when I stopped going down.

I gave him my watch and told him to give me a call once I'd been down 20 minutes, then to pull up the hose as I came up.

Bless him. He told me we shouldn't really be doing this, that he wasn't trained to be a dive supervisor. I never told him that my diving medical had run out about 15 years ago and I shouldn't be doing it either. I wasn't in the mood to debate, so I jumped into the ocean.

So much for black water, it was clear as a bell. I could see for miles. Down I went until, just before the bottom, I spotted one of the divers. He was sat on the pipe doing nothing, looking at his watch, converting the seconds into cash the longer he stayed down there. No wonder the project was doomed from the outset.

I picked an old bolt up and sneaked up behind him. I banged him pretty hard on his helmet and bubbles flew everywhere. He turned round and saw me waving and shouting. I was sure I noticed some brown dye coming out of his suit. I could see the diver talking to the surface and pointing at me.

A lot of good that would do him – the supervisor never knew I was down there. A little voice in my helmet said '20 minutes', followed by, 'Do you think he can hear me?'

'Take your finger off the button you knob and I'll tell you that I did.'

Maybe he had been telling the truth when he said he wasn't a trained dive supervisor.

Later they made me promise never to do that again. Poor lad nearly had a heart attack and told them that I was trying to kill him. He even told the crew that they should watch out for their own safety!

When asked why he was sitting there at the bottom of the ocean doing nothing, he said he'd been waiting for something to come down the down line. He obviously wasn't expecting that something to be me.

The job went much quicker after that day.

I was threatened that if I did it again, they'd report me for not having a diving medical.

What a bunch of arseholes.

All I needed now was a nice break away in peace and tranquillity. Although, sometimes they say, 'Be careful what you wish for.'

26

Hell

I N 1993, Rockwater thought it would be a good idea to send the senior managers on a week's course in the countryside – do some bonding and learn some management skills at the same time. After Taiwan I needed a relaxing setting and this, in theory, sounded like it could be just the ticket.

Countryside? It turned out to be an outward bound adventure school in a place called Ardmore in Scotland, in what was considered to be one of the most inhospitable places on earth. The school was run by none other than John Ridgway, whose claim to fame was rowing across the North Atlantic in a 20-foot open dory called *English Rose III* – in only 92 days. He then went on to sail around the world in the *English Rose IV*. His CV, combined with the setting, was telling me this was not going to be my idea of relaxation.

On the first day they made us walk all the way up a hill which nearly killed me. Our aim was to find the guy who was going to be our team leader for the next few days. Once we'd found him, we would walk all the way down the other side and look for a canoe in the reeds.

I felt like Moses.

Once we found the canoe we had to paddle out to an island, take all our clothes off, get back in the canoe, go out into the middle of the lake and turn the canoe over. Then, we had to escape and come up doing an eskimo roll. I'm not kidding when I say the water was *unbelievably* cold. I ended up with three Adam's apples. I was used to getting into freezing cold water with a suit full of nice warm water. Deep sea divers are tough, but we don't like the cold. I'm not sure what this was supposed to achieve. Seems no one was able to tell me either.

Once everyone had done this, we got dressed and went looking for our tent which had been hidden. With the help of some near useless clues, we eventually found the tent several hours later. We then had to blindfold one of the guys, who was then instructed by another manager to erect the tent. It would have been a lot quicker without the blindfold.

By this time it was getting late, so we lit the camp fire to get warm, cook our supper and deter a few mosquitoes.

Supper was a real five-star feast. It came in vacuum-sealed packets that we had to mix with water in a pan, then heat up in a pot on the fire. We then rubbed the mosquito repellent on each other, at which point it officially became teamwork.

With dinner ready, we now really started to get into this whole bonding thing – one big pan of food, accompanied by only one plate and one spoon. This basically meant we had to pass the plate round and take a couple of spoonfuls from the spoon that had just come out of the last person's mouth. In my case, this happened to be my mate Smudger.

Smudger, based on his surname being Smith, used to be an engineer back in Aberdeen and had come offshore with me once or twice. He'd since gone to Norway on a job, fallen for a pretty young blonde and got married. He was indeed a good mate. However, on this occasion he was sporting a massive cold sore on his lip which was bubbling and weeping. Pop me 500 feet below the ocean with sharks – no problem, but when it comes to using things that have been in other people's mouths with a dollop of their saliva hanging off it, I'm a bit finicky.

After the feast, it was bedtime. I was sharing a two-man tent, with two guys who were massive. Somehow I ended up in the middle and within minutes these two turned their backs to me and fell asleep, only to then let loose with a farting orchestra, which I had the joy of listening to in stereo. Great. At that precise moment, I was already looking forward to the time to get up.

When the time did come for getting up, I thought, 'At least things can only get better.' Wrong. 'How would you like an early morning dip in the Atlantic?' they asked. 'Followed by another rollover in the canoe?' This time, however, we stayed in the canoe and with the help of the instructor we turned the canoe back the right way, via yet another eskimo roll. Such great fun. I couldn't wait for my breakfast. I had egg, bacon, and sausage in my mind, with a luxury bonus of HP sauce.

We ended up having pre-packed porridge mixed with water which was passed round on the plate we'd had the night before.

I found a flat bit of wood which I used to eat mine. Smudger asked if he could share it. I told him to use the spoon like everyone else.

The instructors were all on leave from some killer unit (read: SAS) and did this for fun. The whole week for the rest of us was a nightmare.

It only became enjoyable when we got to Ridgway's proper camp. They had wooden chalets which were nice and warm with our own beds and in the evenings, his wife and daughter would do the meal.

Everything was sourced and/or produced on site: fresh lamb, salmon, mussels, pork. Those ladies certainly knew how to cook, as it was always delicious. We were also allowed a glass of wine. However, as we couldn't get away from the team-building, we had to talk to each other during meal times.

Every day started with either a swim or a run. I didn't like either option.

Once he found out I'd been a diver, Ridgway thought it'd be a good idea to teach the other members of the team how to dive. He had some old diving equipment. I took one or two down without too much drama, but then one lady panicked.

When we got down to about 30 feet, I turned and looked at her to give her the thumbs-up routine, ask if she was all right, that sort of thing. But when I looked over, her eyes were big and scared, full of fear. I noticed her mask was slowly filling up with water and she was starting to panic. The water had just gone past her nose when she finally panicked, big time.

Remember, panic kills.

I got hold of her and we headed in the right direction and at the right speed. When we hit the surface, she spat the mouthpiece out, ripped her mask off, and was trying to scream. Luckily her mouth was full of water and no sound came out – just the water she'd swallowed.

I hate noise.

There's an old expression – an artist is not necessarily an art teacher. I'm not saying I'm an artist, but I was certainly not cut out to be a teacher.

Though I vowed never to return, six months later I did it again. I must have been mad. The second time I did it was even worse because I knew what was going to happen. It was more like a survival course than a team-building course. I'm still not sure just how effective these things are in the real world.

I say we all did it again – all bar one that is. One of the guys nearly died of exposure to the rugged conditions, so he gave it a miss next time round. Although exposure was the key word on his return to his town. Little did we know, but that first course was filmed and aired on Channel 4. After that programme, he ended up getting his own little fan club.

A week was a long time walking up and down mountains and swimming in ice cold water, but I'd got to like Ridgway and he liked me, so I invited him to come offshore for a few days at a later date to see what it was like. He said he'd love to, and with a shake of the hand, I got on the bus and headed back to Aberdeen.

27

Madame Guillotine

TRUE to my word, a few months later, in early 1994, I arranged for Ridgway to join me and the crew on board a vessel called the *Regalia*, in the middle of the North Sea.

The job was a routine one – putting a subsea manifold in. Instead of pinning it to the sea bed with round piles and hammering them in through the legs, we were going to use skirt piles that went round the outside of the manifold. It was a new system to us and required a different kind of hammer.

We called this new hammer 'Madame Guillotine' because it was shaped like the old fashioned guillotine. We'd sailed from Peterhead with the manifold and Madame Guillotine on board. The divers hadn't gone into saturation at this point so they had a chance to look things over and make sure they understood how it worked. It was a big advantage if you could see it on the deck. Normally, the first time you'd see things is when they were hanging ten feet above your head, bouncing up and down underwater.

In order to ensure I was able to reciprocate Ridgway's kind hospitality, I got him a nice cabin with a VHS player and knowing how much he detested Don Johnson, I left him one video – *Miami Vice*. He simply wasn't a *Miami Vice*-type of guy. Revenge was sweet.

Ridgway was up on the bridge drinking a nice cup of fresh black coffee talking to Ulf the Swedish captain when we left

Peterhead. Ulf had done the course as well, but only once. Smart guy that captain.

On the way out we passed over the place where a fishing trawler had sank on its way back to Peterhead a few months earlier, with all hands lost. I told John the story.

I'd finished working offshore at the time of the sinking and was working in the office. When I heard of the tragedy – and because of our relationship with Peterhead – I'd offered to collect the trawler and all its lost souls next time we passed with the vessel. It was well within the capability of the barge and it would have been a nice thing for us to do for the people of Peterhead.

My secretary came into my office with a flushed look on her face and said a well-known Scottish politician, who will remain nameless for this story, was on the phone. I told her I was busy talking to my mate Porky in Singapore, and asked if he could hang on a minute. She disappeared, only to reappear five minutes later, this time looking a bit stern. She told me he was still waiting. I could see she was cross. Her face always went red. I said goodbye to Porky and hello to the politician.

'I understand you've offered to recover the trawler for nothing?' he said.

'Yes,' I said.

'I think it's too dangerous,' he went on.

'No, it's not too dangerous. We can do it easily,' I replied.

'Are you qualified to do this sort of thing?' he asked.

'I reckon so, seeing as this is what we do for a living.'

'Well,' he said, 'I think it's too dangerous and I forbid you to do it.'

Those politicians sure knew a lot about salvage.

'It's a pity for the relatives,' I said. No reaction.

I later saw on the news that they'd given the recovery to a Dutch company that used a totally unsuitable barge to lift it. The barge could only work in flat calm weather. Unsurprisingly, for the North Sea, it spent most of the time waiting on weather. I think the final bill was £4m but I'm guessing there'd been some political gain. After all, those guys never do anything unless they are the main benefactors.

One word does come to mind when I think of this particular MP – prat.

Back to the subsea manifold project.

The crew, on this job, were mostly regulars, consisting of a mixed bunch from around the world. I'd told them which ones were going into saturation first and the LSTs were getting the chambers ready for blow down.

Old Ridgway liked talking to the divers, possibly because they had something in common – most likely a lack of common sense. We spent many evenings exchanging tales and were both fascinated with each other's disciplines. I couldn't come to terms with how or why he would want to cross an ocean in a tiny yacht, especially when on occasions I found it bad enough on a huge ship. On a similar parallel, he was fascinated with how divers lived and survived in tiny chambers for a month at a time, with their only outings during that time being underwater. He asked me to share some anecdotes.

I told him the story of the diver who was looking for a leak on a pipeline we'd been testing a few months earlier.

When pipes had had any kind of remedial work done on them, they'd already been pressure tested to check their integrity. A 24-hour test normally took about 36 to 40 hours depending on how quickly the pressure stabilised. Once it was stabilised, it had to be held for 24 hours.

It was a pretty simple operation really. We filled them up with coloured water so if they leaked, the diver could spot the water coming out of the leak. The pipe under test was at full pressure, but there was a slight pressure loss so we needed a diver to check the areas most likely to have a leak.

The ROV had detected what was, most probably, some coloured water coming out of the flange on the end. On closer investigation we found there was some seepage coming out of a little plug in the middle of the flange. A bit of a shit really, because the pipeline would have to be depressurised and the plug removed, re-taped, and replaced. The line would then have to be repressurised and the test restarted.

As was the nature of some divers, he thought he'd just put a spanner on the plug to see if he could tighten it. That plug had enough pressure behind it to blow his head clean off if it came out, though the silly idiot must have forgotten that. We could see what he was up to via his hat-mounted camera because, next minute, he was looking straight at the plug with a big spanner in his hand and a hammer. Before he could be stopped, he hit the spanner with the big hammer as hard as he could and – BANG – the plug came flying out followed by a big stream of green dye.

Luckily for him the plug missed his helmet by a fraction, otherwise it would have gone straight through his head.

As a result of shock, he suffered a minor heart attack and had to be recovered to the diving bell. That was the end of his diving career.

I know what he was trying to do: save time and money on retesting. His sentiment, if not his common sense, was in the right place. The subsequent investigation cost a quarter of a million pounds.

I turned to Ridway to reassure him. 'These events don't tend to occur that often. I'm sure this job won't be anywhere near as colourful.' Famous last words.

It was an 18-hour steam to the work location in the North Sea, so everybody had a chance of a bit of rest before we got there. It was always a good thing to have a briefing with the deck crew, divers, and engineers. We even used to let the client rep attend, if we knew he was okay.

Client representatives were the people who represented the company you were working for. They included ex-divers and engineers. Sometimes you had one of each. In some cases the diving reps were known to us. A fair way to describe them would be, when they did dive, they never got put into saturation much. Saying that, they knew all the rules. I guess you could call them back seat divers.

The good ones were a great help, especially if some of the work procedures had to be changed on site or you needed stuff transported out from the beach in a hurry.

The weather forecast was fine on the work location, so the divers were blown down into saturation. The job was quite deep – 400 feet at operational depth – so we blew them down early so they could get themselves sorted out before we reached the location.

I say the job was quite deep, but just to put the 400 feet into perspective and also show how insignificant we are in relation to ocean floors and depth around the world, listen to this. When the *Titanic* went down, it sunk 12,500 feet (over two miles) to the bottom of the ocean. It could have been worse, as certain parts of the ocean sink to depths of almost 40,000 feet. I almost ended up working on salvaging something from the *Titanic*. More about that later.

For this job, I'd decided to put a couple of South African lads in, a couple of Scousers, and a few others. One of the Scousers had recently worked with us. A right nutter, but a good laugh.

A few weeks earlier, he and a few mates had gone to a nightclub only to be rejected at the door by this big bouncer. Normal folk would go elsewhere, but not this lad. With very little ceremony the Scouser grabbed the guy by his balls which he was squeezing fondly, while cooing in this guy's ear that he'd like to come in and bring his friends with him. The bouncer agreed and let them in. Getting out was a bit trickier as, by that time, the bouncer had found some mates. I don't think anyone had told the bouncer and his mates that Scousers don't seem to feel any pain nor do they bleed easily. Thankfully, no harm done, and nobody suffered more than a few cuts and bruises.

The Scouser went down into the chambers on his arrival back and it was business as usual. The other divers going included one of my brothers and a few of his mates.

We arrived on location in the North Sea and had the same hassle with the DNV guy. DNV was the company in charge of insurance and risk management, and had responsibility for the manifold's safety. We had to sign a form of release so we could cut the sea fastening and lift the thing off the deck and stick it in the water. They always thought the sea was too rough so the captain and I would have to convince them it was quite calm.

Our vessel could stay on location in 80mph winds and we never put the cranes down until the wind was blowing 60mph. I even remember still having the bell down when the wind was gusting at 83 – although that certainly isn't a recommended standard of practice.

It all depended on the vessel power consumption and footprint (the circumference of movement of the vessel) and I always listened to the captain. If he said it was time to quit, it was time to quit.

The DNV man would look at the wind speed and the state of the sea, and then ask me what I thought. I'd always say 'it looks fine'. Well, let's be fair – you can't get on with the job unless the manifold is on the bottom. I knew my deck foreman would be able to get the manifold off the deck safely seeing as I'd trained him.

While this was going on, the surveyors on the bridge would have set their acoustic transponder array on the sea bed and sorted the manifold landing spot. It would show a box displayed with blue lines. The manifold would have transponders on it that would show a red box. When I lowered the manifold into its final position, the red box had to be inside the blue box.

It was a good system and worked ten times out of ten, so long as the transponders didn't fail. It also meant the divers didn't have to be anywhere near the manifold until it was on the sea bed. Manifolds going up and down near the sea bed caused quite a lot of suction, which created a mud cloud resulting in bad visibility. It was always nerve-wracking having a couple of divers working underneath.

Two minutes after we got our DNV signed certificate, the burning torches were alight and cutting the sea fastenings. The boys knew the story with the certificate and I would often give them the nod an hour or so early to make a start on cutting the sea fastenings. The DNV man always seemed a bit surprised at how quickly we were ready to do the lift.

Jimmy, the deck foreman, would always check that he was clear to start the lifting operation. There were a few things to check, such as: were the bridge crew ready with the ballast and were we in position? I'd be on the bridge, so a couple of nods and up and away the manifold would go.

Jimmy was getting quite good at this now. By the time it was over the side, he'd only managed to knock a few railings down. Lowering a mass into the water had its critical moments hence the DNV man's presence. It needed to be lowered through the splash zone without letting the lifting slings go slack. Slack sling syndrome could be very nasty, especially for the crane. Slack then snatch could do the crane a lot of damage. Cranes had been ripped off their pedestals before now, that's why they put the crane driver's cab away from the boom. If the boom went over the side, at least the crane driver lived to tell the tale. Crane drivers had died, sitting next to the boom on the bottom of the ocean. Things soon changed after a mishap.

A broken boom is one thing, but if the slings break and the manifold breaks free, it's a year's work down the drain plus another year to build a new one, so we didn't like the slack sling situation. We much preferred to get this part just right.

We never put the bell down until the manifold was close to the bottom. Things that dropped in the water never went straight down.

With the manifold close to the bottom, the deck foreman's job was over – it was now down to me and the surveyor to set the thing down. When I first started I thought surveyors were all drug addicts. Whenever you asked anything they always seemed to reply with, 'I need a good fix.'

'Are we in the box?' I'd ask.

Again they'd reply, 'I need a good fix.'

It was later I discovered they had to wait for their equipment to confirm the signal it was receiving from the transponder was a 'good fix'.

There was a lot of noise in the water and signals could get distorted. Consequently, conversations used to go like this:

Me, 'Is that a good fix?'

Surveyor, 'Wait a minute.'

Me, 'Was that a good fix?'

Surveyor, 'Wait a minute.'

Me, 'Is your fucking equipment working?'

Surveyor, 'You never get any better do you?'

Me, 'Is that a good one?'

Surveyor, 'YES!'

Me, 'Down on the crane.' I used to like saying that.

We'd then have to wait and see if we landed in the box. One thing I never got tired of was being in the box.

Once the mud had settled, the surveyor would confirm we were in the box. The company rep would agree and sign it off. The divers would then go in and release the slings. Meantime, Jimmy and his men got Madame Guillotine ready with a sheet pile. The divers had finished de-rigging the slings from the manifold and were ready for the first pile.

The first couple were complete. It looked like a good system. You'd lower the hammer and pile down. It would slide into the appropriate slots on the manifold. Once it was in and locked, the diver would ask the surface to activate the hammer and it would knock the pile into the correct depth. All in all, it seemed like a good system.

The bell had been down its full six hours, so these divers had done what was considered the normal time for a bell run (the time needed to launch and recover a bell), so it was back to the bell and back to the chambers for those guys. A good day's work over.

This vessel, being state of the art, had two bells, so the other one would have been on the bottom and at least one diver out to relieve the guy who was already working down there. This meant this system was capable of keeping two divers on the work site 24 hours a day making us far more productive than back when I first did it.

In those days we only had one bell so the guys had to leave the work site, go back to the bell, and return to the chamber. The new bell team would have to do the bell checks before being lowered to the sea bed, lock out of the bell, find the work site, and get himself sorted. On a good turn around, it'd take the best part of a couple of hours, three times a day. Forty-two hours a week of wasted vessel time.

Today, the bells are bigger and it's the norm to have two divers in the water at any one time. The North Sea has never been famous for its good weather, so to save two days a week by having two bells down at once was fantastic, especially if we were doing a fixed price job, which most of ours were.

The next two divers in the water were the South Africans. Though these two didn't seem to have any fear, I often wondered if they ticked all the boxes when it came to common sense.

The first South African had set the hammer in the slots and asked for the hammer to be activated. The supervisor told him it was hot which meant, in underwater terms, it'd been activated but nothing was happening. They checked it out on the surface and reported that it should be working.

I was on the bridge when dive control called and asked if I'd go down and see if I could sort things out.

When I opened the dive control door I knew something had happened. The dive supervisor had his 'stay calm' voice on and was talking the divers back to the bell. He put his hand over his mic when he saw me.

'It's not good,' he said. 'Booty's hurt himself. We've got to get them back as soon as we can.'

The engineer waved me over to the TV monitor. The ROV replay showed everything that'd happened. Initially things looked good, with Madame Guillotine in position. However, although the anvil was up, it was stuck. The diver, for some reason, swam under the hammer and looked up to see what was wrong. At this point the hammer released itself and there was an almighty scream that sounded like a dog howling in the desert at night.

The hammer had bounced off the guy's helmet and hit his arm, slicing it off. The ROV showed the moment it'd happened. There was just a puff of colour in the water from his suit. The other diver in the water had seen the incident and was going to the diver's assistance but the guy was in survival mode and had got himself back to the bell. Diver two was helping him but his breathing was out of control. It was confusing for a while as to which diver had been injured.

It turned out the one who'd had his arm cut off was in the bell in a state of shock. I guess you would be if you'd just cut your arm off.

Before the bell could leave the bottom, everything had to be stowed correctly to allow it to pass through the moon pool. His arm was still in his suit but you could see it was longer than his other arm. He was sitting very still.

I'd seen dead people at this stage as part of my job, but this affected me far more because it involved emotion. Blood flowing, screaming and limbs hanging off was enough to get your attention.

The boys in the chamber had been warned things were not good, and that they should be ready to help when the bell was back and locked on to the system.

The recovery was quick and the bottom door swung down so that Booty could be lowered down into the chamber. The guys below remember him being lowered down with his arm hanging loose. They cut his suit off so they could look at the damage and see what could be done. The arm was held on with a couple of sinews.

One of the LSTs was a paramedic. He was talking with the doctors on the beach. They had a special unit in Aberdeen called the National Hyperbaric Centre (NHC) which had an on-duty doctor.

It was possible to send a helicopter with a decompression chamber out to the vessel, lock it on to the dive system, transfer the injured diver into it, put the chamber back into the helicopter and send the whole thing back to the NHC. They could then transfer the diver to a bigger chamber with a doctor who could then take charge of the situation.

Our predicament was not suitable for this. You couldn't put this guy into a small chamber on his own as he would have died before he had reached the beach. Instead, we decided to fly a doctor out to us, where he'd be blown down in our dive system and see what he could do for the diver.

Meantime, the LST had been told to give him some antibiotics and make him as comfortable as possible. He didn't look too good to me – the man was in a serious state of shock and had lost a lot of blood.

The helicopter with the doctor arrived quick time, in just under an hour. On the way down to the chamber room where he'd be blown down, he was brought up to speed on the situation. We locked the doctor in and 20 minutes later he was on the bottom – 400 feet below. That's a hell of a quick blow down – about three and a half hours quicker than normal – but the situation was far from normal.

It turned out the doctor had never been deeper than 100 feet in his life, neither had he breathed gas. When he stepped out of the chamber he'd been blown down in, he was literally trembling. To be blown down to that depth, that fast, his nervous system would have still been twitching along with his hands. The effects he was feeling were similar to that a bounce diver with a bell would often experience, due to not having a great deal of free time at depth and needing to get back up quickly due to the depth.

I don't think he knew he was going to be in saturation for two weeks. I thought, 'I hope he's on a good rate.'

The man was a bloody marvel. He saved the diver's life without a shadow of a doubt. He severed through the sinews which were holding the arm on to Booty's body, cut the arm off, shot him full of antibiotics and bandaged him up all within eight minutes of reaching the bottom. Despite this, it was still touch and go for a few days. We couldn't start the decompression until the doctor was happy that it wouldn't kill the guy.

In the meantime, we were told to make our way back to port by the office, but to transfer our equipment to another semi-submersible vessel that was in the field. The other vessel was one of ours, so the captains had a chat and decided to get as close as possible and transfer equipment by crane.

The sea was getting rough but it was okay. Ulf was happy.

The two semi-subs closed in on each other. It was Swedish nerves against Dutch nerves, two great big vessels like that in the middle of the night drawing closer and closer to one another. The radio kept up a running commentary:

'You all right over there?' asked the Dutch captain.

'Yes, fine,' Ulf answered. 'A little closer please, so the crane can reach.' Ulf was always polite.

The Dutch captain sounded nervous but drew closer. He was the sort of man who could crush your hand with a single handshake.

'Closer,' said Ulf. I think he was testing him.

Ridgway, who was on the bridge, said he'd never experienced anything like this before. What a day for his first trip offshore.

What a day for us all.

He later said he thought Don Johnson was a pussy cat and, subsequently, threw the video into the sea. Funny what you remember.

The arm was sent to the surface and put into the deep freezer. It even had its own shelf. The health and safety man was on his way out for the investigation. We did another bell run on the site to recover the equipment before we could leave for Peterhead. The new team of divers had done a survey to establish what had gone wrong. It turned out Booty had got the hammer and pile in the wrong slots, which in turn twisted things enough to make the hammer jam and, unluckily for Booty, released itself just at the wrong moment.

All dives were voice recorded just in case of an accident. Divers also wore hat-mounted video cameras and we had the ROV video recording. The dive supervisor kept a handwritten log of the dive so we had all the information required for an investigation. The diver's helmet was saved. It had a nasty scratch on the side which, most probably, saved his life.

The only reel-to-reel tape recorder on which we could replay the diver's voice was in the ship's gym. I played the tape a couple of times before the health and safety man got involved, just to go through things in my own mind and to be satisfied we'd done things correctly (which we had).

What I couldn't get used to was that scream. It sent shivers down my spine – still does now every time I think about it. I wondered if the health and safety man would be up for this. He turned out to be an old diving friend of mine called Vic.

Vic had been out to another accident where a lad had been killed, though, like me, he wasn't keen on the tape recording either. Suffice to say, he gave us a clean bill of health.

The operations manager flew out the next day, a Scot. We got on well. He also came from a farming background. His parents had a sheep farm just outside Peterhead. I'd never been sure if it was true what they say about shepherds and loneliness but Duncan seemed quite normal. Saying that, he did have a picture of his favourite ewe in his wallet – that did worry me a little.

We were well away from port, so when he left, it was decided he'd take the arm ashore. No one liked the idea of it staying in the ship's meat freezer. When it was time for him to leave we put the arm in a double black bin liner and off he went. He rang me later that evening, to tell me that when he was going through the heliport in Aberdeen he got a lot of funny stares. It wasn't until he got stopped at customs to ask what was in the bag that he realised the fingers were sticking out the bottom of the bag.

I think that took a bit of explaining.

He certainly wouldn't have made it past customs these days. You can't even bring a piece of fresh fruit into the country, never mind a human arm.

When Booty's decompression finally ended, I was at the chamber door to meet him. He put his good arm around me and insisted on a photo. We had one taken together with the man who saved his life.

The company fixed him up with a mechanical arm at vast expense which he never used. He was often seen driving around Aberdeen with just the one arm. You would have thought one accident would have been enough for him.

Years later I heard he'd invested some of his insurance payout on a boat and shark cage in South Africa where he was doing great white shark spotting. I wondered how many people asked him if the missing arm was the result of a shark attack that he'd survived. It would be a good story to tell down the pub.

Mr Ridgway left saying he'd had a most enjoyable trip. He asked if it was always like this. I told him you got good days as well.

I went on leave shortly afterwards, although it was touch and go if I'd make it home in time as a result of the job spilling over the original timeframe. Thankfully, a couple of days later I was pushing the baggage trolley through the airport whistling and trying to unwind, when the wife said, 'Will you stop whistling? Whatever is the matter with you?'

'Sorry dear,' I said. 'I will try not to be happy.'

I rarely discussed work with my wife, as it was essential for me to switch off. Whistling helped me get into neutral gear, whereas it got on my wife's nerves = still does in fact!

I stopped whistling. One bad trip was enough for me.

28

Knock Me Out

NOT that long after Booty had his arm sliced off, one of my other crew members almost lost his life in a nasty accident. It was Jimmy. The very same Jimmy who had been on board when Booty lost his arm.

He had been with me for a while. He initially started as a rigger and then worked his way through the ranks. He was one of those guys who showed a bit of flair, more enthusiasm than normal. It wasn't long before he became my deck foreman for a big job on a construction barge. He was the main man on the deck and to put it bluntly, you don't fuck with the deck foreman. He was not the sort of guy who would lock himself in an office, instead, Jimmy would be out on the deck with his men, wearing his big jacket and cracking the whip. Although he may have seemed a bit harsh to his crew, he ran a tidy deck, which was very important to the safety of everyone.

This is what happened.

I was standing on the bridge at midnight (sounds like an old film) looking out at the deck. I used to find it was a place I could relax. During the summer it was incredible as I'd managed to see the Northern Lights on more than one occasion.

On this particular night, the sea was rough but nothing serious. Jimmy was moving stuff about with the crane, getting the deck set up for the job we'd just started. He had a container on the crane wire and was skipping it across the deck when a larger than average wave went through, making the barge roll more than normal. The container skidded further than he'd intended. Suffice to say it took him by surprise, hitting him, pinning him against another container. The barge rolled the other way leaving Jimmy flat on his back on the middle of the deck.

I left the bridge and ran over as fast as I could. When I reached him, you could see he wasn't a happy bunny. His whole leg was squashed and his boot had been flattened by the container. Rig boots have steel toecaps and his was flat with his foot still inside. I can't even imagine how painful this must have been.

There was a bit of blood on his boiler suit trousers so, with his rigger's knife, I cut his trousers to see how bad it was. Good job the knife was sharp – he must have had four layers on.

All the time he kept shouting, 'Dave, tell me it's still there.'

'Let me have a look Jimmy.'

What I saw didn't look good and would have made many people retch. The muscles had popped out of the back of his thigh.

'Don't worry, your leg's still there,' I told him. There was no point in panicking him out even more. He was already in shock and he didn't need to go over the edge and go unconscious. I did think, but didn't like to say at the time, 'I don't think you'll be getting your leg over for a while.'

I never tried to remove his boot. I sent one of his lads to fetch the first mate from the bridge. He was the man who was in charge of the medicine room and, at the time, was supposed to be a paramedic.

Turned out he didn't want to get involved. This was not the moment to make that decision, I thought. Bad timing, but something told me that he was probably just a first aider and not a paramedic. Big difference.

It was different learning on a dummy in a nice warm room compared to a wet deck in the middle of the night when it was pissing down with rain with a guy screaming his head off.

All this time Jimmy was holding my hand, shouting at me to knock him out.

'You'll have to let go of my hand for me to do that,' I said. 'Besides, I don't think people would be too impressed if they spotted me belting the shit out of you.'

One of the divers came over and told me they were trying to get the first mate to get some morphine, but it turned out it was a two-part mix morphine and he could only find the key for one of the cupboards.

Both parts together were effective as a painkiller, but as separate solutions, they were useless. The intention of splitting them up in different locked cupboards, was to deter anyone stealing it and either using it to fuel a habit, or to sell it on. Sad but true.

It seemed like forever before he found the second key and the diver came back with the needle. I only had my t-shirt on and was getting really cold. Jimmy still had a hold of my hand so there was no way I was going anywhere – despite being so cold I could have dialled a phone with my nipples. In the meantime, the diver injected Jimmy with the morphine. It did the trick and he let go of my hand.

The company rep who'd witnessed this had called Aberdeen for the medical helicopter to come as soon as possible. We'd got Jimmy on a stretcher by this time and were carrying him to the helilounge.

The helicopter arrived just as we were going up the last flight of stairs so we carried on up and put him straight in the chopper where the doctor could take charge.

That night, a new deck foreman was born. He had Jimmy's radio. Luckily it hadn't been damaged by the container.

It always takes an incident to change things. After this, we always had a dedicated medic on board. A proper medic.

After the job I went to see Jimmy in hospital. He was looking good. The muscle had been pushed back in and sewn up. His toes had been badly crushed and broken but they said he would be back at work in about six months.

On leaving I said, 'You still want me to knock you out?' Let's just say the second word of his reply was 'off'.

A few months later while in The Dickens pub in Stavanger, I couldn't help myself. I said to Jimmy, 'You want to hold hands again?'

'Fuck off,' he said. 'I've found someone new.'

Bitch.

Keeping upbeat during times of crisis was an essential part of the industry I worked in, simply because crisis happened frequently. However, the next scene I was off to, took the wind out of the most hardened divers' sails.

29

Spooks

CERTAIN dates stick in your head, such as birthdays and Christmas. However, 28 September 1994 stuck in my head for all the wrong reasons.

After the usual morning routine of walking downstairs to put the kettle on and pop some toast into the machine, I turned on the television to hear what was happening in the world, and then walked to the fridge to get the milk for my coffee. With my back to the television, I remember hearing one word, 'wreckage'.

I walked back to the television, turned up the volume and stayed standing as I watched and listened to what had happened about five hours earlier that day.

There'd been a ferry heading across the Baltic Sea from Estonia to Gothenburg, that sank in the middle of the night. The ferry was called the MS *Estonia*, was Swedish and in the early hours almost 900 people died, making it one of the worst maritime disasters of the 20th century.

Large waves had reportedly pounded the gate at the front of the ship continually, and as a result of a failed hinge, water entered the vessel and eventually the MS *Estonia* in under one hour was 275 feet below the surface. Outside of wartime, it was the biggest disaster to ever happen in the Baltic Sea.

As I was watching the events unfold on the television, I was thinking, 'How very tragic. That's going to be one hell of a body recovery and vessel salvage job for whoever takes that on.' A few days later I got the call.

It just so happened we had a Swedish commercial manager who was well connected with the government and had a vessel working not that far away. We also had a connection with a very competent and renowned Dutch salvage giant, so we got the job of doing salvage and body recovery evaluation.

After the Chinook disaster, we'd been given a number of nicknames, one of them being 'The Body Snatchers'. Not my choice and certainly not a great claim to fame, but that's what we'd been called.

Here I was, in Stockholm military airport with my new Dutch salvage expert, waiting to meet a couple of Swedish pathologist policemen and a counsellor to help the lads (my diving team) get over the trauma of what might be waiting for them.

The Scandinavians all spoke excellent English. The Dutch guy wasn't bad either. He also seemed like he'd been there and done that, got the t-shirt. His job was to evaluate how easy it would be to salvage the whole vessel to the surface. The Swedes wanted to see how badly the bodies had decomposed in the time they'd been in the water, which at this point was about six days, so, my job was to evaluate how easy it would be to get anything out of the vessel and recover all the bodies.

Lastly, we would have a look at the front door of the ferry as this is where the experts thought things had gone wrong. Great, more 'experts', I thought.

I suspect they'd thought this because another ferry had sunk a few years earlier for the same reason (MS *Herald of Free Enterprise*, 1987). I was very close to working on that disaster also. I received the call, and with passport in hand was ready to head off, when I received another call to say they had sourced a local company.

Back to the *Estonia*.

Sailing without shutting the bow door properly is not good practice, though this ferry had got a lot further than the harbour – it was in the middle of the ocean. There'd also been talk of a door pin failure. These were the variables for this disaster which we had to evaluate.

The Swedish Navy didn't mess about with survival suits and videos. You grabbed a life jacket and in you went as the helicopter was already running. They didn't even seem all that worried about shutting the door.

Along the way we'd inherited, what would appear to be, a fairly high-up person as he got lots of salutes when he joined us. He turned out to be the government liaison. Why do we need a government liaison man, I thought.

These boys didn't seem to worry too much about altitude – any lower and we'd have needed to lift our feet up.

Out of the window I spotted the semi. We flew round it half a dozen times before they gave the thumbs-up from the cockpit to say we're going to land. Down we went. No fuss.

'Hello, captain.' We shook hands. Gees, I forgotten what a grip this guy had – almost brought tears to my eyes.

I got together the relevant people who needed to be involved in the meeting. As the divers were not yet in saturation I decided it'd be best for them to hear straight from the police pathologists what they'd be looking for.

The government man showed them a drawing of the location of the door pins and what they should look like in the closed position. The salvage guy just said, 'We'll play it as we go along, depending on what we find while we're looking about.'

We did know that the ferry was lying on its side, so from the port side to the starboard side which was lying on the sea bed, would be about 90 feet high. The plan was to get inside by means of either breaking into portholes or cutting an entry into the hull.

Portholes would have been quicker, which on these boats were as big as a house window, which gave lots of room for the divers to get through.

One diver would go inside, with the other diver sitting at the entry point tending his umbilical. This way we knew how much of his umbilical was inside, giving us a good idea how far in he was. Once inside, we'd evaluate the condition and see how far in the lads could get from any of the entry points.

It sounded like we had a plan to be getting on with. If necessary, we could modify it as we went along.

The government liaison explained the wreck had been buoyed and a guard boat had been on location. If it hadn't have been, the wreck would have likely been plundered by Eastern European ex-military divers who had the capability to do it. This guy seemed to know more than he was telling.

The talking was now over. It was time to get the divers into saturation after a quick chat with the counsellor about what to expect. Although the lads didn't want to hear the talk. They wanted to get down into the chamber ASAP, shut the door and start the blow down.

In their minds the talk was wasting time. They weren't naïve – I think most of them knew it wasn't going to be pleasant inside the ferry but would cross that bridge once inside.

As usual the ROV was first down, doing a survey of the hull, looking for any obvious points of entry to save time once the divers got down. Because of the decompression problems, the divers would start at the top and work down. Ninety feet was outside of their upward-downward excursion range. ROVs don't have that problem.

The government man was keen for the ROV to go and have a look at the condition of the front door and its locks. As we had time, before the divers would be out in the water, we had a quick look. As there was no door, an inspection of the locks was easy. We showed them what they wanted to see – some broken locks.

Government man then asked if we could see anything suspicious. The ROV operator explained he could see as much as we could. Smart arse.

I said we'd be able to have a better look with the divers but asked him if there was anything he was looking for in particular.

'Signs of sabotage,' he said.

I'd never dealt with any blatant attempts of sabotage before. The closest I got was looking for a bomb which the Royal Navy was trying to locate somewhere off Teesside. We never did find it.

With almost 900 dead, foul play certainly couldn't be ruled out here.

Breaking the portholes proved to be difficult. Using a sledgehammer in the middle didn't break them. It turned out that, if you hit the pane of glass right in the corner with a spike, you could break it. Following that with a blow from the sledgehammer and we were in.

Once all the sharp pieces of glass were out of the way, in went the diver nice and slowly, being tendered by his mate on the outside.

I wondered what the diver was thinking when he entered the hull. After all, who knew what he might have found? He was one of our lads and had been on these kind of jobs before so he was part of the unofficial 'body snatchers' crew.

On the surface we were all watching the pictures from his hat-mounted camera. There were several monitors dotted about the semi: a couple on the bridge, one in the client's office, one in my office, and the one in dive control. We installed lots of monitors so people didn't have to keep going into dive control and pestering the dive supervisor.

Inside the ferry, the diver said he had managed to get inside one of the cabins. Wearing a camera on his helmet, we could see that the cabin was in a right mess, with debris floating all around. He had no idea which cabin it was. He couldn't open the door to the corridor which we figured had been locked from the outside. With our new breaking and entering skills we decided to try again.

Trying another porthole, the diver entered another cabin and this time, bumped into a half-naked woman and a fully dressed sailor wearing a pair of big yellow gloves. God alone knows what had been going on in that cabin.

As before, the cabin was a mess with more debris everywhere. The diver managed to unlock the door and open it. He managed to get some way down the corridor but couldn't find a door he could open. Retracing his steps, he got back to the porthole.

In our brief the Swedes had said that no bodies would be removed until they requested it. It was a case of one out, all out. If we couldn't find them all, the harsh truth was that their grave would be the bottom of the ocean.

If the bodies were to remain inside, one idea that'd been discussed involved covering the ferry in a concrete blanket to keep the looters and pirates out. It's sad, but a reality that has happened since the beginning of time.

The second plan entailed salvaging the ferry and removing the bodies when the ferry was towed to the designated berth. We wouldn't be part of that job.

As we needed to get further inside, a new plan was developed. Through comms and cameras, we advised the divers to cut their way in through the hull using underwater burning equipment. Our location was to be the main stairwell leading to the bar and reception area, because this was the largest open area and where we were most likely to find the majority of the bodies.

The lads were holding up well. They didn't need the counsellor. If anything, he seemed a bit put out. I told him it was early days yet. Though, I was never sure quite what he thought he'd say to people who'd been trained by the SAS and served time in violent hotspots around the world. They could have probably offered him a word or two of advice.

Burning took a bit of time as these ferries had a double skin hull, but we got there, and finally in the right place.

As the images from the cameras started to clear up, there was a sobering silence as we could all start to make out what was in front of the divers. We'd found dead people. Lots of dead people.

Every time the diver moved his head camera to show us a different angle, it was like a freezing bucket of water was being dropped over each individual in the room I was standing in. There was a lot of sighing, a lot of people putting hands over their mouths in horror and many shaking their heads and pacing the room.

As the divers continued with the task in hand we witnessed kids still holding their mother's hands, trying to avoid the crush of people as the mad panic began. Most of them were at the bottom of the stairwell. They looked like they'd been desperately scrambling to try to get up the stairs to the main deck. The scene of them attempting to pull themselves up the big slippery brass handrails either side of the stairs, while the pressure of water had thrown them back down and rapidly drowned them, looked like it was frozen in a snapshot. At the time of this happening, it would have been deafening with screams, shouting and water rushing in. The silence now spoke volumes. I'll admit that I got numb.

When the water started coming in, the boat listing to one side together with the now slippery handrails meant the people would have had no chance of getting up the stairs, as was obvious with the amount of people floating about.

The inside of the bar area was devastated. The ceilings were all false and had collapsed, furniture was everywhere and basically anything that was moveable was floating about. It was carnage.

It was certainly too dangerous to let the diver go too far inside. Going into the unknown with their umbilical in tow, anything could have happened and I wasn't going to risk it.

It was time to show the police pathologist one of the bodies.

The diver got hold of a kid with long hair who was floating nearby. He must have been around 14. He held him up so the diver's hat-mounted camera looked straight into his young face. On the barge, all the monitors – the bridge, dive control, offices – showed the same grim picture of this young kid's face.

The pathologists seemed happy with what they'd seen. One sighting was going to be enough. I'd also noticed quite a few monitors had been switched off. That face must have stayed with a few people for a long while. It did with me, especially as my kids were about the same age.

The counsellor went very quiet. I don't think he was expecting what he'd seen. I had a word with him. He seemed okay, but I knew it was an emotionally fragile situation when there I was counselling the counsellor.

There was no way we could get to the other side of the ferry to do any body recovery, so it was decided to halt the body search, focus on salvage evaluation, and check the door locks.

It was now salvage man's turn. He just wanted to see how the ferry was laying on the sea bed.

Recovery of boats requires buoyancy and lifting equipment. The more buoyancy you can put on the sunken vessel, the easier it is to lift. We did this via massive air bags. In this case, buoyancy would be put on the lower section first to level the boat on the sea bed, then equal buoyancy all over to keep it level. Providing you could get some lifting equipment attached at a suitable place, you could then start your lifting operation.

Once you'd got it up to the splash zone you could put giant salvage pumps into the hull and wait for the ferry to float again. For a moment my Dutch mate had me convinced that it could be done. Thing was, I'd remembered just how long it took them to float a fishing trawler off the coast of Peterhead.

At the same time the ROV was doing the survey, the divers had gone to the bow of the vessel to check out the locks for sabotage. To me they looked like they'd just been ripped off. When the door had gone there was no sign of any red or black wires taped to the hull, nothing at all suspicious. In fact, the weld around them looked pretty new.

Most of the pictures were taken for the government man. He then asked if the divers wouldn't mind going inside to assess the state and nature of the vehicles and their cargo.

Again it was a mess. I told the guys not to go too far inside as I didn't know what the lorries had in their cargo tanks. It could have been toxic. As no one could tell me what they were carrying, as far as I was concerned it was a no-go area.

Finally, we were asked if we could get inside the bridge, which we did. The captain's hat was where it should have been – on his head. A black box equivalent they were keen to locate proved elusive, even after a good search.

I asked them if they were happy with all the information we'd gathered for them which was met with a unanimous 'yes' and a big thanks to the divers for performing a difficult and most unpleasant task.

Much later, I heard there'd been a report which had been done by one of the Swedes. It seems they'd seen a bottle of whiskey being locked in the chambers of my divers. This was being frowned upon and was, apparently, becoming a bit of an issue. When asked if this was true, I vigorously denied it. I'd lost my bottle of duty free, though I never did work out where that went. I'd just assumed the counsellor had nicked it.

My leave had been cut short to do this job, so when the Swedes asked if I'd like a ride back to the beach in their helicopter I immediately accepted. The Dutch guy and the counsellor also flew back with me. By this time, I figured he'd also had enough.

Back in Stavanger I had a chat with the Swedish commercial manager. He told me there were all sorts of rumours flying around about how the disaster had happened. Some said the ferry had been sabotaged by the Russian secret service because it was carrying military equipment. The truth is, nobody ever did come out with a definitive answer. It seemed obvious that the gate was the reason the ship went down, but the genesis as to how it became vulnerable was never established.

He also asked about the whiskey. I told him I had no fucking idea and asked why such a big deal was being made about a bottle of whiskey, especially in the face of what had just happened. Apparently it had come from various religious groups who thought it was bad to have drunk divers around the bodies. It's no secret that divers like a drink off site, but under my watch, on the job, we were sober as judges. I explained, for what it was worth, that I never lost my bottle until the job was over.

Back in Stavanger we were on the news. I had to go and have my picture taken standing next to a diving bell before I could go home. Once back home, looking at my teenage son – especially with that young lad's face still fresh – I became rather upset.

For about three years I received phonecalls from various parties claiming to do research on the real reason the ferry sank, asking if they could interview me, if there was anything else I could remember. I didn't fancy fueling their conspiracy theories. A lot of people had died in this disaster and I'd played my part to assist. I declined and moved on.

30

Life On Mars

B Y the mid-1990s, I had my routines down to a tee. Knowing I was going to be away for a while, on the morning of my departure I'd turn to the wife cap in hand and say, 'Come on, I'm gonna be away a month!'

'Oh well, if you're quick then.'

Who said romance was dead?

Another month's leave over, I said my goodbyes to the wife and children and made my way to the airport ready to catch the red eye flight to Stavanger via Schiphol, where I was off to join a decent crew on a commercial diving boat in Norway, ready for another job. These were guys I'd been working in diving and construction with for many years by this point. Good years, but tough. After all, you don't get many pussy cat divers.

Every one of the lads was part of the family but you did have your favourites and having globe-trotted with him for 20 years, Eddie was one of mine.

Eddie lived near me and we knew a lot of the same kind of people. He was a man's man, as they say: big guy, real joker, bit of a rebel and a good drinker who told lots of funny stories.

People would say about me, 'Here he comes with his minder.'

I kept Eddie's secret for him. Like a lot of big guys he'd never hurt a fly.

When he first started he'd cut his teeth as an air diver and by the time he worked with me he was a sat diver. Although, at times he was a better pub diver (big drinker) than salt water diver, but I guess that could be said about a lot of us. I know where I'd have rather drowned.

As I pulled up to the airport at Norwich, Eddie was there waiting for me, ready to lock into autopilot on a journey we'd done several hundred times before.

I'd used Norwich airport for years. I reckon I was one of their first customers. It's very convenient. A short drive from my house, a quick 45-minute flight and I was in Amsterdam – gateway to the world. On the return journey, with the time difference, it was as if the flight never happened, as I'd arrive 15 minutes before I'd left Amsterdam.

On early flights the planes never had heaters. The stewardesses would call you 'dear' or 'love' and give you a blanket if you were cold. They'd spread them out on your lap then nip you on the cheek to see if you were still alive. If you twitched, they'd give you a drink. Nowadays, you get a biscuit and a glass of orange juice and you don't get hyperthermia.

Amsterdam used to be a great duty free shopping area until they joined the European Union and cancelled all our rights. I used to buy a half gallon of gin. The bottle was huge. When customs in Norwich asked if I had anything to declare, my reply was one bottle and two hundred cigarettes. I got away with it for years until one of them looked in the bag and said, 'My, my, what a big bottle *that* is.'

Game over.

We landed in Schiphol. The taxiing took as long as the flight. You knew when you were getting close to the terminal as you taxied over a bridge that crossed a busy road which had lorries taking tulips and balls of that cheese with red stuff around it from Amsterdam to goodness knows where.

The plane came to a halt and we disembarked on to the bus that was waiting a short distance away on the tarmac, just far enough to get wet.

Schiphol is a great airport and once inside it's warm. Dry, too. Finding your way about is easy and in no time I was in the executive lounge. Still too early for a beer but I suppose a small glass of champagne didn't do any harm with some of those smoked almonds. Trouble is, they were salty and you needed some serious willpower once the salt had kicked in not to go for a few refills on the liquid refreshments.

The stewardess with the blue uniform shouted, 'The Stavanger flight is boarding.'

We hurried to the boarding gate ready for the next flight. Just my luck, a seat looking straight out at the propeller: Pratt and Whitney. How many times had I seen that.

The flight was full, the air con seemed to be broken and the guy sitting next to me seemed to have eaten a whole garlic clove and lost his toothbrush. Still – only two hours to go.

Cheese seemed to be the staple diet on KLM airways, which despite loving cheese, was not great for me as it would always bung me up. Thankfully I was able to mix it up with the balance of the gourmet offering of salted almonds, Heineken beer, a bread roll, fresh fruit, a strong coffee, and another sneaky Heineken.

We droned on until *ding ding* – 'Fasten your safety belt, lock your service tray away, and put your seat in the upright position as we'll shortly be landing at Stavanger airport.'

On arriving at the airport, we jumped into a taxi that would take us to the office. It was a nice big Mercedes, with an anti-smoking policy inside the car, which meant it smelt fresh. Back in the UK in those days, it wasn't strange for the taxi driver to pick you up with a fag hanging off his bottom lip and as you pulled opened the door, it looked like a scene out of the film *Backdraft*. We arrived in Stavanger in record time, although it seemed to me that the driver had been going far too fast on the snow-covered roads. It was not until later I learned they were on winter studded tyres which they'd put on long before the snow came.

Can you imagine us Brits being told we must have two sets of tyres: one for winter and one for summer? We're only just getting to grips with having a decent tread on them. As opposed to the UK, I don't think the Norwegians depended on councils with lots of gritting lorries with no grit.

We had a nice office in Stavanger. The people were great, warm and welcoming. It was customary to visit the project manager before going offshore. On this particular day we were meeting a man called Jens, who was a great guy and spoke excellent English. Handy that, as my Norwegian was a bit patchy. I found that 'yes' can mean 'no' when nodding your head up and down and vice versa when shaking your head. It took a while, but was okay once I'd got the hang of it.

They tended to do big projects in Norway, due to the water being deep. Consequently this job would need to be engineered well, so I always sent a few engineers over from Aberdeen to give them a hand.

A few nods and shakes later and the meeting was done. Time to relax for the evening.

Norway is what I always thought Mars would look like – minus the wooden houses. I started working there back in 1980 and soon established that it was not a bad place once you got used to it.

Most wooden tops (Norwegians) made their own alcohol with their private stills, due to a bottle of house wine costing seventy quid back in those days and a pint of beer £6 – at a time when beer was about £1.50 in the UK and a half decent bottle of wine was about £5. It was however illegal to make home brew, as alcohol was banned in a lot of the land, so they had to do it behind locked doors and definitely not on a Sunday (or at least until after church). They mostly got it right and it kind of tasted okay, but there had been a few fatalities. The lads stuck to the six pound a pint stuff.

Same went with cigarettes. It seemed that all Norwegians smoked back then. As cigarettes were so expensive, they rolled their own, which were far more potent and stunk the room out. The mindset of the Scandinavian governments was to make smoking and drinking so expensive that everyone would give it up, in order to make them opt for a healthier lifestyle – while saving the countries several millions on medical bills. Not sure how well that plan worked out though.

I'd arranged to go out for a meal with Smudger that night, to discuss the pending job and of course, catch up on the good old times. Smudger always seemed to pick nice restaurants, and although I was glad to see they had steak on the menu, I felt guilty and had the fish. You had to have the fish really when in Norway. The only thing I refused to eat was whale meat. I think they should stop killing whales.

After dinner we stopped at the best-known pub in Stavanger, called The Dickens, to see if there was anyone in there we knew. You could normally bet on seeing someone. For the younger lads, they banked on it. They even went as far as renaming it 'The Dick-Ins'.

The pub was nice and warm but full of smoke. It would usually take a while to spot the person you were meeting. If I hadn't known better I'd have thought the place was on fire.

There were a few old faces in the pub that night. Smudger said there'd be some more of our crew in later on. Looking around, I could see a Norwegian had passed out, rendered unconscious through alcohol and his mate was lightly running his lit cigarette over the unconscious guy's lips making them twitch. How nice it would be, I thought, to have a mate like him. On that note, I thought it might be a good time to move on and leave everyone to their £6-a-pint merriment.

My hotel was only a five-minute walk. As it had a nice bar inside I thought I'd have a cheeky nightcap – a nice cold glass of wine before bed.

The SAS International hotel in Stavanger had several floors which had different themes. I think it was supposed to give the place an international feeling. They couldn't have had many Japanese in that night as my room was on the Japanese floor. If you like loads of bamboo and beds that look like mats, you'd have probably loved it. Still, it did the job.

I had an early shake organised, ready for my taxi to the heliport the next morning. I hated early morning wake-up calls but I did like hotel breakfasts: crispy bacon, poached eggs, fried bread, mushrooms, and tomatoes with lashings of HP sauce.

Unfortunately, you didn't get that here.

At this hotel, you could have an egg boiled for one, two, or three minutes. They even had labels telling you how long the egg had been boiled. I'd tried them all and, to be honest, they were all hard. Your soldiers bent when you went for the dip.

They had cheese with nice bread. Jam, too. You could even have smoked cod if your stomach could handle it first thing in the morning. I couldn't risk it as I was going on a helicopter in a couple of hours' time. I opted for toast with jam as I don't think they had ever heard of Marmite.

As I arrived at the heliport, I paid the taxi driver and checked in for my flight to the semi-submersible diving barge which would be my home for the next month.

After check-in, I headed to gate number one. I showed the lady my bags and said, 'No ma'am – no alcohol, no lighters, and no drugs – just me. I'm not a terrorist, just a construction manager.' Looking mortified, she told me to collect a survival suit and proceed to the pre-flight briefing room. Nowadays, I would have probably been arrested at the mention of the word terrorist.

Into the briefing room I went, watched the safety video and then boarded the craft. Up we went with a little wobble, while the pilot got his balance, then nose down and away over the fjords we went. It was spectacular. You saw all the wash from the boats which seemed to be going in every direction. The Norwegians were (and still are) a nation of boats owners, and why not when everywhere is connected by water. And if you didn't own a boat, hydrofoils and ferries were never far away.

For this job in 1996, I was working on board the *Regalia* vessel. A tunnel about a mile long had been built under the sea as it was easier than trying to bring a pipeline ashore over the cliff and rocks. The client had dug this tunnel out to where we had finished laying the pipeline, laid a pipe in the tunnel and dug a vertical shaft up to the sea bed.

On the top of the vertical pipe was a cap which protruded on to the sea bed. Our job was to install a plug into the top of two riser pipes. The plug turned out to be so heavy we had to make a special frame on the front of the barge to hold them, which still had to be partially submerged to take some of the weight off them.

The plug might have weighed 500 tons but it had to have a very soft landing. The plug, once lowered down, was not allowed to bounce up and down on the pipe protruding from the shaft that came up from the tunnel. Precision was the name of the game, with no deviation for error.

It all sounded like a good plan but I'd never been offshore when the weather was good. In fact, there was always a two-metre swell and the vessel would be going up and down whatever happened. Even with the heave compensation on the crane, it was always going to be a bit tricky.

Still, we said we could do it and I was shown how this equipment was going to make life easy. It was quite simple really. It showed the rate of descent for the plug and it showed the stationary bit on the bottom of the sea. All I had to do was watch the monitors from the bridge and remember these barges didn't just go up and down but had a movement circumference of three metres. You got quite a pendulum movement which got worse when the vessel moved.

The plan was good. We were going to lower the plug until it was five metres above the target then, at the right moment, we would seize the opportunity and lower the plug with divers assisting below. Once we'd made contact, which I could see on the special equipment, the crane would lower as fast as it could. This would have a big effect on the stability of the barge which, in turn, would ballast to counter-react so as not to turn over. I asked the captain if he was happy and he responded with a nod.

We always operated with an ROV, which relayed everything that was happening back to the bridge. I planned on using the ROV to rotate the plug to align with the spools. In front of me was the special equipment, which consisted of an electronic map of the sea bed, a picture from the sea bed comms to the crane driver, a line of sight to captain and 12 company reps sitting behind with orders to be quiet.

We'd had dinner, so I figured we might as well get started. It was a one-off shot, as when the plug was removed from the frame we wouldn't have been able to pick it up again. I gave the order to the deck to cut the plug free and for the crane to get it away from the barge as fast as he could. I didn't want the thing smashing against the hull making big dents or possibly even piercing it, which in turn would take the vessel down.

Once it was away from the boat and on its way down safely, I thought this was going to be a piece of cake and stopped sweating. 'All stop!' I shouted as it was five metres off the sea bed. It was time to take stock of the situation and get the vessel in the right position for the final phase of the lowering. Everything checked out, people were all happy.

There was a monitoring system in the tunnel which could see how soft the landing was. Orientation of the plug was critical as special spools had been fabricated to join the pipe to the plug. At approximately the length of Wembley Stadium, these spools were the biggest in history at that point in time – another first. Bearing in mind its size, I reiterated to everyone again that precision was of paramount importance.

It was now time to get off the pot, come down easy on the crane and be ready to come off the load as fast as we could when we bottomed out. The captain was ready to hit the ballast pumps and I was looking at the special equipment to make sure it went into the right place. Three metres to go and looking good, two metres to go and looking good, one metre left and the special equipment screen went blank. I thought, 'Fucking typical!'

This is when you earn your money, having to make a decision while not discussing the status quo with the reps. I was thinking, 'Come on Stefan – shift some water!' I looked at him and he had gone a bit white but Stefan was a good guy and had the pumps and crane working flat-out.

This plug weighed 500 tons – roughly that of 40 double decker buses. Stefan looked to be standing at a funny angle but in hindsight it was the angle of the deck due to the weight of the plug. The 12 company reps had gone very quiet, with a few of them wiping beads of sweat from their foreheads. Then the crane slowed, the barge started to level out and the reps began to clap as we had set a perfect plug. The report from the tunnel said it had only kissed once and did so perfectly. Pretty rare stuff.

I looked at Stefan and he now had the colour back in his face and smiled. I said, 'You okay?' He replied with 'yar yar' (Stefan was a Swede). He asked inquisitively, 'Is that what it said to do in the procedures manual if the screen went blank?' I replied, 'I think that page was missing.'

The reps never knew what happened and thankfully the Scandinavians were a liberal bunch who didn't ask too many i's to be dotted or t's to be crossed. Unlike the next bunch I was about to work with.

31

Union Rules

IF you wanted a big project then you did what was called a high deck installation. I was about to embark on one of these in 1997 in a place called the Wandoo Development, 80 kilometres north-west of Karratha which is well north of Perth – a godforsaken place with nothing but red earth.

I'd done several projects Down Under and from my experience, it was not the easiest place to work. They had serious issues with their unions. The last job drove me near to insanity. Here's what happened.

We mobilised a boat out of Singapore and the entire English crew had to be replaced by an Australian crew, which was simply due to the union dictating this. The officers were great, as long as they did what the seamen told them to do, then things would go 'fair dinkum' as they'd say.

We had two captains: a regular one and an Australian captain, who both arrived on the same day. The crew, on the other hand, had to arrive two days earlier so they could acclimatise. This time was normally spent in the bars and clubs. I didn't feel sorry for them. If they were unfortunate enough to get pissed and turn up for work late, they could not be held responsible. Union rules would cover them.

When they did arrive, there were so many things they weren't allowed to do as a result of union rules, that I began to wonder if we'd actually be able to get the job done. As it turned out, the officers would give us a hand if needed. The dive superintendent was a grisly Australian but not a bad guy. He brought his own dive team, as they did, which consisted of a high proportion of New Zealand Maoris – great big fellows. I did wonder at the time if we had diving suits big enough for them as they genuinely looked like the national rugby team's scrum.

Problems arose when we realised the dive system's escape capsule on this vessel wouldn't be big enough to hold them all. I asked for smaller divers but apparently they didn't have any. In the end we did manage to overcome the problem, as the inspector agreed we could use the diving bell as a second rescue chamber.

I decided to grease the inside to make it easier and sent a small diver first so if one of the big ones got stuck they could pull him and push him at the same time. It was always good to have a system.

We made good time, despite a failed pirate attempt halfway through the trip which we foiled. A ketch boat pulled up tight beside us, but the captain went full steam ahead and they gave up after a short while. Option B was certainly not in their favour as the captain was looking to slow down and release the anchor on to their boat. I did think about asking the New Zealanders to put their diver's knives between their teeth and do that dance they do before a rugby match which always frightens the Scots. Thankfully it never got to that stage.

We had a brand-new big yellow state-of-the-art ROV, which cost £14m. It was a bit over the top but the company wanted to test it.

The dive crew had had lots of meetings on the way down, with the likes of the crane driver and the guy from the flexible pipe company, so I was confident they'd be okay. In fact, these were the only two important people we needed. I wasn't getting good vibes from the riggers, but the captain and his first mate said they'd be all right on the day.

The job itself was easy enough – just lay a flexible pipeline from a loading buoy in the middle of the ocean to a subsea wellhead a few hundred metres away.

I sent some riggers over to the buoy ready to lower the pre-installed winch wire down to our rubber boat so we could hook the wire to the end of the flexible pipe. That done, the pipe was pulled over the stern and up inside the buoy ready to lay.

At this point we were stuck – tied to the buoy until we had finished laying the pipe.

Great, especially as it was now lunchtime and we all had to return to the boat and stop work for lunch – union rules.

'You've got to be kidding?' I said. 'Can't we have lunch in shifts?'

'No,' came the reply.

So they all came back for lunch. They got one hour exactly. As the ROV crew weren't in that union it was okay for them to work.

Over the side went this state-of-the-art ROV, only to break its tether when it hit the water. I could see it bobbing about just below the surface, but it was moving away in the tide pretty quickly. There was only the crane driver about. I asked him if he'd come with me in the rubber boat to recover the ROV. He agreed, but only if he could drive the boat. It was like dealing with children.

Off we went in pursuit of this state-of-the-art ROV which, it seemed, only I was concerned about. The crane driver had brought his VHF radio so we could call the boat and let them know we were in pursuit of the runaway ROV.

We caught up with our runaway and managed to get a tow rope on, fastened it and started back towards the boat. The amount of revs required to make any headway pulling this thing into the tide was too much for the little outboard and the sheer pin broke on the propeller. It was at this point we realised we didn't have any tools or a spare sheer pin.

Our big boat couldn't come to our rescue as they were securely tied to the buoy. Besides, it was still lunchtime.

We were now drifting helplessly in the middle of the Timor Sea which was full of sharks with the sun beating down.

'No worries,' said the crane driver. That was another expression they used a lot. It normally meant, 'You're in the shit – big time', and this time was no exception. As the radio didn't work, all we could do was wave and by this time we seemed miles away.

Assessing the situation, I realised I was in this little rubber boat wallowing about in an enormous ocean with no communications and a crane driver with a red spotted bandanna who kept saying, 'No worries, mate.' It was getting hotter by the minute and we had no water. By this time we'd lost sight of the boat. I had no idea what was going on back there.

I figured someone would wonder what had happened to us and send the rescue boat. I didn't think I could listen to many more stories about this guy's experiences on Bondi Beach with his Sheila.

Just as I was going delirious from having no water, too much sun, and an overload of Aussie anecdotes, the lifeboat from our vessel arrived, full of jolly faces. The chief said they'd not been able to start the lifeboat. That shouldn't happen, I thought, it's a lifeboat. They'd been guided from the main boat that had kept us on the radar screen.

Back on board, the ROV crew thanked us for saving their machine. The crane driver was given a bollocking by the union representative, as not only had he missed his lunch, but it wasn't in his brief to leave the boat in the middle of the ocean.

Not a lot went wrong after that. We had a bit of a moment at breakfast when one of the seamen asked for some Vegemite which we didn't have and instead I offered Marmite or raspberry jam as alternatives. The little shit turned to me and said, 'I don't want Marmite or jam, I want Vegemite and I'm entitled to it.' In the end we agreed to log it in the ship's log as a serious breach of union rules and they agreed to go back to work. And I'm not joking!

I made a mental note to kill him if I got the chance.

Back on deck, things were going well. We'd only managed to get one twist in the pipe which we called the Chubby Checker so that the company man didn't know what we were talking about. The divers could fix it later so there was no point making a fuss about it at this point.

The big boys were doing well on the sea bed. There was a lot of grunting and heavy breathing but the supervisor seemed relaxed. This job would be over in no time and, sure enough, after a function test and an ROV survey, it was over.

On the way in, we were asked to stop and pick up a helicopter from the sea bed which had been there for about three days. It was an opportune stop as we just happened to be going past this particular stretch of water.

For some unknown reason, the helicopter had needed to ditch when it had malfunctioned. It looked fine on the sea bed when we'd surveyed it, but by the time we'd bashed it on the side of the vessel a couple of times it was a wreck and would never work again.

Another story for my mate on Bondi Beach.

A helicopter was sent to take all the riggers and non-essential personnel back to the beach to get them off the payroll as soon as possible, all the way back to Singapore. Company policy. No point keeping them on board. I took the opportunity to go with them. I'd gotten a good sun tan on the way down.

The wife never liked me coming home with a tan when she was white. She used to think I'd just been lazing around in the sun. Technically for a short time I had been – albeit on a rubber dinghy in shark-infested waters drifting off into the unknown.

On board the helicopter, the guy flying it was wearing a blindfold. I was fast beginning to see how the other one may have crashed. Sat in the co-pilot seat was another pilot. He explained to us the pilot was doing his instrument test and that he'd take over if anything went wrong.

No worries mate.

I remember thinking 'let me out' but he actually did okay and we managed to take off and land safely.

We landed right at the top of Australia where the Timor Sea joins land. It was full of saltwater crocodiles and was just a short hop from Darwin. We stayed overnight and then caught a charter flight down to Perth the next day.

Darwin was a bit of a one-horse town that was still recovering from being knocked flat by a tornado a few years earlier and was very humid at this time of year. Thankfully, the hospitality helped take our minds off the backdrop. That night in the hotel restaurant was my first time eating a crocodile starter, followed by a buffalo steak for main, washed down with some fine Australian wine. Just to make sure I looked the part, I bought an Australian Akubra hat – but without the corks. After all, I didn't want to look like an idiot.

At the airport the next day, we left Darwin and jumped on a flight to Perth. The lads looked a bit rough as they'd stayed at a two-star hotel and from what I can understand started drinking with some of the locals, who could have turned drinking into an Olympic sport.

Our plane wasn't very big. It was company policy not to overspend on travel and with this 16-seat carrier, they'd certainly ticked that box. No toilet or cabin crew.

The lads – and you can't blame them with a long trip ahead – faced with the prospect of no beer, decided it was time to go shopping. They called tins of beer 'stubbies', and they'd got plenty enough for the flight. Possibly even a few too many.

Up, up and away to sunny Perth we went.

The lads were popping the tins like there was no tomorrow. After all, I'm sure there was a clause in the union handbook highlighting the need to get pissed while on a light aircraft with no toilets.

From Darwin to Perth, you flew over the Newman Desert for miles and miles. The lads popping those tins soon discovered that our company policy cheap plane had no toilets. So, what do you do when your bladder's bursting? Piss in the empty stubby tins. Soon we were faced with more urine than empty tins to which the lads decided the solution was to piss in their boots. Messy, but a solution.

It never crossed their minds to stop drinking the stuff.

In the end, the pilot had to make an unscheduled landing in the middle of the desert at a sheep station. Bladders empty, it was back on the plane. Clear the sheep off the runway and away we went, with only another three hours to fill the tins and boots again, which they duly did.

I was glad when we landed in Perth and found a proper toilet. I am British, after all.

They had to leave the windows and doors open on the plane for a day before they could charter it again.

I don't know why but I always had this opinion that Aussies were rough and tough, a bit like how Crocodile Dundee is portrayed in the movie. All I can say is it must have been the crocodiles that found them tough.

From my experience they were hard going – but not tough. While reflecting on this job, I was now *really* looking forward to the Wandoo assignment.

32

My New Best Friend

BACK to Wandoo – I knew it was going to be a challenge if we still had issues with the unions. The job was in two parts – literally. Build the gravity base south of Perth in a place called Bunbury and the deck section in Singapore. Once the gravity base had been built they would tow it out of the dry dock where it would be stored. It would then be towed to the location and we would ballast the thing down until it was in position on the sea bed, before filling it with iron ore as a permanent ballast.

Once the deck section had been built on the quayside at a shipyard in Singapore, it would be skidded on to a barge that had been fitted with a bunch of winches for mooring it when we got to Australia. The deck section weight alone was around 7,500 tons.

In the North Sea it would have been lifted off the quay, set down on the deck of a DP lift barge, taken out to the location, lifted off the deck and lowered into position. Maybe 12 hours' work. However, they didn't have anything like a crane barge in Australia. To take one down from the North Sea and back would have cost almost as much as putting Neil Armstrong on the moon.

As with most things in the oil business, there was always an engineer with a calculator and a draughtsman with a pencil, who, with the help of an ideas man, could come up with a solution. In this case, the solution was called a 'float over'.

It was not the first time it had been done elsewhere on the planet, but I was about to be one of a handful to do it. Certainly the first one ever in Australia – unions allowing. Another first! I must stop saying that.

This project required a great deal of commuting between the UK, Singapore and Perth in Western Australia. My first visit was to Singapore and turned out to be fun. I inherited my new best buddy who used to be my old worst enemy.

I'd first met Dale through another guy called Vince, whom I'd worked with in the North Sea on the same barge doing joint venture jobs. We'd do all the diving-related work and they'd do all the deck fabrication stuff. It should have worked well. Problem was, we could never work out who was in charge. They thought they were, but we were really.

We sat in the same office with the same-sized desk and the same amount of staff. Our cabins were almost the same size or, at least, should have been. Mine was bigger. This didn't sit well with Vince, even though we tried to make my arch rival's cabin as comfortable as possible. We even gave him a table lamp.

Vince had a terrible reputation for hiring and firing people and a nasty manner on the VHF radio.

One day another boat, bringing us vital equipment, called the barge. Vince answered the radio. A very polite captain said, 'Hi, I'm bringing this equipment you require – what is your location so I can be with you as soon as possible?'

Vince being Vince, and not being very clever, replied, 'We're in the middle of the ocean, asshole,' and changed channels.

Vince's henchman Dale clapped when he heard this. What a nugget, I thought. Luckily the bridge crew had heard the conversation and managed to calm the supply boat captain down to a level where he promised not to come on board and kill Vince.

Vince would always answer his telephone the same way: *Ring Ring…* 'Vince's phone' – he would then have his conversation, mutter a few words of wisdom and hang up. One night Vince died. It was very sad – nobody clapped. We believe he died of a broken heart because his cabin was so small. He was pretty needy.

I heard his phone ring a short while after he was discovered dead, only to hear the nugget answer, 'Dale's phone.' They hadn't even got him in the bag when his treasured phone had been taken over by his successor.

Dale and I had the same battles as I'd had with Vince. Now he was going to be my new best friend on this job. This time though, it was going to be different – he was definitely working for me.

Whenever we met, we'd always talk about good old Vince, saying things like what a great guy he had been, but the reality is that he wasn't loved by many.

Dale had lived in Australia with one of his many wives. He had a ranch with horses and some sheep, so he qualified as an Australian. However, shortly after, his wife took the ranch together with a new lover and Dale was back on the road looking for a new job. He was somewhat unlucky with women. By this time he'd had about five wives and each one had taken all his money and left him skint.

Dale had been anchor foreman on one of the big barges in the North Sea and this job required a good anchor man, preferably an Australian. Better the devil you know and in all honesty, once I got to know him, Dale was alright.

We needed 12 big, reliable winches – which was a lot of winches. It would keep him busy and out of my way, as it also required a lot of legwork going round all the places in Singapore that hired out. As for me, I was off to Australia for a meeting with the oil company and a game of golf with a mate of mine.

Singapore airport was one of the best you could ever use. I arrived at Singapore Airlines check-in, when the girl behind the desk asked if I had a visa to enter Australia. I asked her if I needed one, to which she told me in no uncertain terms that I did. I told her I'd have to call our travel department to see what they'd done about it. After a quick phonecall I went back to the girl and told her there'd been an oversight and that I didn't have a visa.

'You can't go then,' she said.

'I must go,' I said. 'I'm playing in the Wandoo Golf Classic tomorrow.'

'My god,' she said. Admittedly, it did sound quite impressive – the Wandoo Golf Classic.

'Let me talk to my superior,' she said.

A short time later, the girl and her supervisor came back with a suggestion that we rang Canberra to find out if they could grant me a temporary visa. The supervisor called them and explained the situation about the golf tournament and how important it was. I had to talk to another lady who told me how silly I was not to have a visa. I blamed Greg Norman.

'Who's he?' she said.

In the end she said I could board the flight but that I would be arrested at immigration in Perth where I'd have to go through the process of getting a visa. She added that this was the first time this had ever been allowed – another first. I promised the girls I'd give them some personal golf tuition when I got back to Singapore.

Sure enough, at passport control I was arrested. It was quite a cosmopolitan experience, as a Scottish guy arrested a Brit in Australia. He thought I was an overpaid golfer and decided to make a right meal of things. He said if it'd been down to him he would have left me in Singapore to miss the competition. Prick.

I eventually got out of there just as it was getting light. I thanked the Scot and told him not to forget to watch the competition to see how I did. He asked me what channel it was on. I told him I had no idea but it should be in colour.

The sheep farmer from Peterhead let me sleep for two hours before he called to say he was on his way to pick me up for our little game of golf and asked if I'd be ready. I asked if we'd have time for breakfast. No, he told me, apparently we'd be having it at the golf club.

He arrived in his Rover 110 – his pride and joy. What a heap. The windows kept falling down, the doors were loose, and the upholstery was cracked but he loved it. We did get some glances when we pulled up at his club. I think most of them were in wonderment that the thing was still running.

Breakfast did help a bit, but I was knackered and not looking forward to it at all. On top of that, he'd put the wrong handicap down – basically one I couldn't play to. I may as well have been Greg Norman.

Playing on the course was novel. I'd never played with kangaroos hopping about and the fact I kept getting constant reminders about deadly snakes in the rough was also very different – especially as I spent most of the day in there.

I'd hit a ball, which in turn would bounce off a rock and then go into the rough. After seeing a king brown slithering off out of the grass, I decided, no more searching in the rough. New balls please!

In under an hour, the sun started to fry me. The back of my legs were like bacon and my neck was starting to blister. By this stage, all I wanted was to go back to the clubhouse for a cold beer.

On the golfing front – we lost, the clients won. What a surprise. Who cared! But I did get to play in the Wandoo Classic. I wondered if the stroppy Scot was still trying to find it on his telly.

I only stayed for a few days – just long enough to have the best oysters ever and watch the worst movie ever. Duncan's Dutch wife took us to an outdoor movie theatre, which turned out to be yet another cosmopolitan experience. A Dutch movie with French subtitles, in Oz. He looked as bemused as I felt. No wonder he divorced her and married a nice English girl from the office.

Next day, we took a scenic trip through Fremantle and down through the vineyards, before finally getting to Bunbury. We'd gone to see how the gravity base was coming on.

The base was nearly finished. The guy in charge told us, within a couple of days they'd flood the basin it'd been built in, to make sure it floated and stayed upright, and that it was fit for purpose ready for its long sea voyage. My new best friend was going to ride on the tugboat that towed it to its final location.

He didn't know this yet, but the episode would eventually turn him into a bit of a hero.

They hit a storm and the tow rope snapped. Dale was lifted by winch from a helicopter and lowered on to the structure with a couple of riggers. With nothing pulling the structure it was drifting and wallowing about, making it quite precarious to lower people down from a hovering helicopter. But, in true Dale style, he did it.

He attached a new tow rope with no thought for his own safety, but he did say afterwards, he was a bit concerned for the men he sent down to the lower deck to do the connection. Someone had to be in charge and work the radio he later told me. He was a real life Crocodile Dundee Australian action man.

They did a great job, especially as the structure had been heading for the rocks. The tugboat captain had gone closer to the shore to try and avoid the weather but the swell had caught him out and, inadvertently, almost caused a major upset. It would have set the project back 18 months. Dale showed me a picture which featured him and had made it to the newspaper. Without showing too much emotion, I was quietly proud of him.

Back in Singapore I had words with our travel department about the visa. They just squinted at me but giggled when I told them the story. In the meantime, the top deck section wasn't due to be skidded on to the barge for a month so I went home to the UK to have a couple of weeks off.

33

More Meetings

WHENEVER we had an incident on a project, everyone and his dog would get summoned to a meeting at the oil company's headquarters. A broken tow rope was an incident, no getting away from that.

It was a long way from Norwich to sunny Perth. Twelve hours to Singapore with a further six-hour flight to Perth. I'd only been back home a week but they insisted I attend.

Singapore Airlines were great. The girls looked after me well, giving me just the right amount of alcohol to make me sleep and just enough water so I didn't get dehydrated. We landed on schedule, had an hour's walkabout in the terminal, then boarded the Qantas flight to Perth.

I'd just finished my glass of champagne when they made the announcement that we'd all have to leave the plane and return to the terminal as there was a technical problem.

The technical problem turned out to be a bomb scare.

They told us to remain in the glass departure room until they'd completely checked to see if there was a bomb. When I asked a member of the cabin crew how long we'd be delayed, she told me she had no idea. I asked if I could go for a walk around the terminal.

'No,' she said, 'you must stay here as we'll need you to identify and check your bags when the plane has been cleared.' Ten hours later I was identifying my bag on the runway before being allowed back on the plane. I did get a couple more glasses of champagne while the rest of the passengers checked and identified their bags. As we sped down the runway I thought to myself, 'I hope they checked this thing properly.' Too late now, we were up in the air.

This time, on arrival, they let me straight through immigration as my visa was still valid. No sign of the stroppy Scot, so it was straight through to the taxi rank. I was only eight hours late for the meeting.

I rang the office to find out what time the meeting had been rescheduled for, only to find out they'd gone ahead and had done it without me. Apparently there was someone more important than me who couldn't wait. I aired, 'So I've flown halfway round the world for nothing?' The response, 'Sorry.' What an absolute waste of time.

I spent a couple more days in Perth but this time I avoided outdoor movies. These kind of meetings make a man question whether this is the life for him anymore. I'd revisit a similar scenario in the not too distant future.

The conclusion, at the meeting (which I did not attend), was to have two tugs when the deck section was being towed down from Singapore reducing the risk of a broken tow rope by 50 per cent – brilliant. All that distance and time wasted in a boardroom to basically conclude that we would have two tugs, just in case one breaks. Apparently it takes a full boardroom to make a decision this complex.

I flew back to Singapore, then with KLM back to Norwich. I did get one of those little Dutch houses full of gin to add to my 95-strong collection every time I flew business class with KLM, so it wasn't a complete waste of time. Although not every house was full – and not because I drunk the contents. If you flew from a country such as Libya you would get a Dutch house, but it would be empty due to alcohol being prohibited in that particular country.

Two weeks later and it was time to skid the deck section on to the barge in Singapore, where my new best friend was waiting. He'd got all his winches fitted and tested, ready for when we arrived in Australia to do the installation. I arrived at the barge and was greeted with a big smile and a hug. Dale was pleased to see me.

We quickly walked around the barge looking at the winches – just what I needed after a 12-hour flight. If winches are your thing Dale had ten nice ones. I knew what was coming when he said, 'Let's go for a beer.' It was time for me to hear his exploits about what happened when the tow rope parted – great.

We went back to the hotel and arranged to meet at the pool on the roof. He beat me to it. He was sat next to this lady on the edge of the pool. They both had their legs dangling in the water looking very relaxed. Dale's pulled, I thought. He had his Akubra hat on, which after a month of intense sweat and god knows what else, had certainly earned that 'broken in' look which he was hoping for.

He waved and told me he'd ordered a couple of beers and to come and sit with him and the lady. She was very nice but never moved even when Dale asked if she'd like a swim with him. After all, how could she turn that down, especially as he'd only shuffled his false teeth round a few times. I'd noticed before, he did that when he was excited. A nasty habit of his – one of many nasty little habits.

The beers came and went. He suggested we went and sat at a table, so up we got. Being the gentleman he was, he held his hand out for the lady to hold. It was at this time we found out she had no legs below the knees. He muttered something completely stupid to the poor woman and we left her sitting on the edge of the pool. What a gent.

Next day it was time to skid the top section on to the barge.

We got off to an early start just in case things didn't work out as planned. We had a sub-contractor who had these big strand jacks capable of pulling far more than the 7,500 tons that the deck section weighed. The boss of the jacking team told me the only dodgy bit was when they had it between dry land and the floating barge. I wished him luck, told Dale to stay out of his way and not to interfere. Oh, and to stop shuffling his teeth.

They dragged the deck section on to the barge. It wobbled a bit when it left dry land. There were a few 'oohs' and 'ahhs' from the onlookers but it never turned over, only rocked a bit. All in all everything went smoothly and it was quickly in its final position ready for the welders to do their bit.

On came the welder to do the sea fastenings. Twelve hours later the barge was hooked up to the tugs and off they went. Next stop; the Wandoo Field ready for the first high deck installation in Australian waters.

I waited in the Perth office for the deck to arrive. We had Dale's crew assemble it in the office and the project engineer went through the procedures as best he could. Dale added his bit which amounted to, 'When I tell you to come up on the winch, you pull the lever backwards. If I tell you to slack the tugger, you push the lever forward. You will all have a walkie-talkie with a spare battery.'

Who needed a massive book with procedures that took 18 months to write? We had a marine crew that would attach the mooring lines. I guess keeping it simple was the best way.

We all left Perth in a fixed wing plane bound for Karratha, where we then jumped into a helicopter and flew out to a nearby rig. On arrival we were lowered down on to a boat, and then in turn to a smaller rubber boat, which transferred us to the barge with the deck section.

We had a kip and some food on the rig, but that was it until the job was done. We had a long day and night ahead. The weather forecast was good, so it was game on.

It was like a crew of pirates scrambling up the side of the barge, but we all made it. Dale had warned his crew about getting their radios wet – it's all in the detail. Once on board, there was a 'One, two, three, testing. One, two, three, how do you read me?'

Same old answer, 'Too loud, too clear, and too fucking often.'

By the time we had the barge moored up in between the platform legs, about 20 client onlookers had arrived. They'd established themselves in what was mine and Dale's control station.

They didn't like it but they left and found a new vantage point. When you had a lot of clients on a job, in turn, you ended up with an awful lot of experts, with an awful lot of opinions. However – when you asked one of them to give the word to start the operation, you could hear a pin drop. They didn't do risk. Didn't take long for me to start dishing out the marching orders to the experts.

The weather was still okay when we'd got the last of the mooring lines attached. I told the welders to start cutting the sea fastenings, which was going to take the best part of six hours to do. During this time, we could tension up the mooring lines, get the barge into its final position and test the ballast pumps – which was done as follows.

On top of the platform legs there were four big cones, and on the bottom of the deck section were four big stabbing pins. We simply ballasted the barge down until the stabbing pins were in the cones, kept ballasting the barge until the deck section was sitting on the platform legs, then pulled the barge out. Job done – a complete platform.

There always seemed to be a new weather forecast just as I was about to start. In six hours the wind was due to pick up. The sea state was about to increase to what the on-board insurance guy would classify as unacceptable.

Time for a chat with him. I told him I had a 95 per cent chance of getting the sea fastenings cut with no chance of re-welding them in time. In my opinion we needed to carry on with the installation. Credit to the guy, he didn't run to the waiting experts for their advice. Instead, he just gave me the nod. Dale put his rigger's knife back in his pocket.

An hour later, with the wind freshening, we began ballasting down. The waves got bigger and the wind had increased but it was still okay. Ballasting is a slow process, but down went the barge. The stabbing pins were just about to go into the cones when Dale radioed me to say one of the mooring lines had just broken, but we should be okay to hold position. This was very concerning.

The pins were almost in the cones when Dale was back on the radio – another mooring line had just parted.

'We're jumping about more now and the barge is moving about with two lines gone. Ballasting up is not an option,' he said.

Then, there was the crashing sound of metal on metal. What a noise it made as the two halves touched. I nearly soiled myself. I looked up and we had three of the four pins in the cones. I knew I couldn't leave it like this.

Just then, there was an even bigger crash of metal on metal. Poseidon, god of the sea, had sent a bigger wave that'd lifted the whole barge with the deck up, then down it came with an almighty crash. I didn't like to look up, but I would have been shirking my responsibility had I not. The entire crew was paralysed as the ocean had now taken control of the labour.

After everyone waiting for a few seconds to assess the outcome, it became evident that all four pins were in the cones. The wave had lifted everything up and out when it passed, and as a result, things had crashed back down into perfect position. On every job you had to have a bit of luck.

Things quickly stabilised from here on in. The tugs pulled the barge out from between the legs and all the experts reappeared who all said, 'Well done.' If they'd been honest, they would have said they weren't expecting things to be quite so noisy and chaotic.

We spent that night on the new platform having a wash and a good kip before going back to Perth for the celebration. It might have been a bit noisy and a bit messy but they'd got their first platform.

Dale and I got separated for a few days. We met up in Perth for a drink and spoke bullshit, which was the ideal recipe to unwind to. Without him the job would have gone to rats. He'd held his nerve, kept his men focused, and his radios dry. What a guy.

I went back home to the UK for some much needed R-and-R, but sadly, a couple of months later I found out Dale had died.

34

Divers Will Be Divers

AFTER making history in Australia with the Wandoo job, my boss wanted me to stop working offshore and consider taking on the role of operations manager in Aberdeen, which would entail me working from an office every day. Although I would still be in charge of diving, I was concerned that I might simply get too bored too quickly working behind a desk.

I enjoyed going places and doing big projects, but I was also aware, being a few months away from my 50th birthday, my priorities in life were starting to shift. By the nature of the last three decades, I'd always be a diving person, but needed a bit of time to reflect to ensure the move would be a prudent one and to consider how enthusiastic I would be in an office capacity. I told him I'd think about it, but wouldn't be making a decision for a few weeks.

I've always found that a great way to decide about the future is to sometimes reflect on the past. Experience has also taught me that a suitable environment to do so can often be a bar.

Soon after the job offer, I was in Stavanger getting ready to oversee a welding job and while looking at the scores of divers coming in and out of The Dickens, it sparked off a few funny tales.

As some of the crews sat down ready to eat some grub, it reminded me of a nightclub, not far from The Dickens, that had a rowing boat in the middle filled with fresh prawns. When you paid to go in, they gave you a ticket which you redeemed for a big jug which you would fill to the top with Atlantic prawns, and some lovely warm fresh crispy bread on the side. It was a great concept, though your hands stunk by the end of the evening.

We got barred once. One of the lads decided to dive from a balcony into the boat and the prawns went all over the floor. Divers will be divers. There was a lot of shouting and screaming. I don't think they'd seen that done before. Wherever we went that night, we made the jumper sit on his own as every inch of him stunk of fish.

Having the crew stinking of fish was not ideal, but getting them there to a job in one piece was more testing.

One night we'd finished mobilising in Leith, Scotland. It was around eight o'clock.

The lads asked me if they could go to the bank, but must have thought I was daft as the banks shut at 3.30pm. However, funnily enough, the pubs were open.

'Okay.' I said. 'But be back at 11.45pm as we're sailing at midnight.'

So 11.45pm came and the captain and I were looking out the bridge window thinking they were cutting things a bit fine, when here they came, fighting a rearguard action against the taxi drivers and the police who are all punching the shit out of each other. 'You shouldn't be punching that policeman,' I thought. 'You could get into trouble.'

This was just another regular night out for divers. A skinful of beer, a fight with the locals and an irresponsible ending 90 per cent of the time. I often used to have an attack of my conscience, thinking, 'I shouldn't have let them go ashore as I knew it would end like this anyway.' Nights like this shouldn't have happened, but they invariably did – again and again.

One of our guys was down and two of his mates were dragging him by the legs. He was face down in the gravel and layers of skin were being sanded down. Never good.

The lads made it back at 11.55pm, so I couldn't bollock them for being late. A big Scottish copper came on board and asked who was in charge. I looked around but, in the end, I had to own up.

We had a chat, although I found this copper's Scottish accent almost impossible to understand, so spent most of the time nodding. I explained that we had to leave on the midnight tide, and despite our north/south communication issues, he turned out to be a good guy and let me off with a warning. I think he'd seen it all before. I explained these guys would be blown down into the saturation chambers the next day and would be down there for 28 days. I don't think he quite got the gist of it but I reckon he liked the idea of them being contained.

The guy they'd been dragging looked a right mess. A lot of skin had gone from his face and there was blood everywhere. He felt no pain when the medic cleaned him up. You could see what six pints of heavy does for you. 'Heavy' – that's what they call bitter in Scotland. The guy was lucky that he made a full recovery before his wife saw him again.

A few bruises, black eyes, a few teeth missing. We had to get those bubbles out of our blood somehow. You have to remember the old divers' saying, 'No sea too rough, no muff too tough, we dive at five!' No idea what it meant but it was on all our t-shirts.

However, on occasions, when things did get out of hand, I had to lay down the law. One time, one of the divers got a bit too drunk and irresponsible, and I had to sack him the next day. When I told him he was fired, he hit me so hard I went clean over the bed that I was standing next to and landed on the one behind. Turns out he'd been an ex-middleweight champion boxer in the navy.

After that, I always kept a bed between me and the bloke I was sacking.

Some other interesting tales would often occur after we'd have our demobs and we were going home via Aberdeen airport. As you can imagine, after 28 days in 'the pot' as it was called, void of any alcohol or nicotine, and no sex, you were ready for the full house. However, divers never seem to learn that a glut of alcohol makes you do silly things – *really* silly things.

One of the lads had to have a sit-down comfort break in the airport. He'd closed the door, as you should, and dropped his trousers which were clearly visible under the door which had a two-foot gap between the bottom and the floor.

His mate, who was having a stand-up comfort break, saw an opportunity and the devil took over. He reached under the door, got hold of the bottom of the trousers and with one big pull, dragged them clean from him. Just then, the tannoy announced the London Gatwick flight was boarding.

Shout as he may for the return of his jeans, his mate had legged it to the departure gate with no intention of giving them back. Final boarding was announced, leaving the guy with no alternative but to leave the toilet and proceed to the departure gate in his underpants.

Luckily the effect of the alcohol was still with him so he brazened it out and boarded, albeit with some strange glances and a few whistles. His wife was not impressed when, after 28 days away, he arrived at Gatwick in his best boxers. I'm not sure he'd have been allowed to board in this day and age.

His mate came out on the baggage carousel holding his trousers. Very mature stuff.

However, the next anecdote I reflected on, was nothing short of bizarre. I was on a job with Smudger in the early 1990s getting ready to mobilise out of Peterhead – a nice place north of Aberdeen, which had a big fishing port. I'd sent the lads up the day before and put them up in a hotel with orders to go to bed early and behave. The orders fell on deaf ears.

I left Aberdeen early. It was only an hour's drive to Peterhead and I arrived at eight o'clock in the morning. I thought I'd have breakfast with the lads before we went to the boat.

The receptionist said they hadn't had breakfast yet but had received their early morning call. I thought, 'I'd better go and wake them up,' just in case they'd had a skinful the night before and had gone back to sleep. It's been known to happen.

The receptionist said they were in room number 69. That's a bad omen, I thought.

I took the lift and eventually found the room and knocked on the door. No answer. I tried the door to see if it was open. When I opened it I was expecting to find a couple of them comatose on their beds. We always put them in double rooms as it was cheaper and they could keep each other company. I didn't want them getting lonely.

There were no lads in the room – only a lady lying face down on one of the beds. She was naked as the day she was born but, unlike the day she was born, she had a hairbrush sticking out of her backside.

I decided to have a closer look and make sure things were okay. I wriggled it a bit but she never moved. I quickly decided some things are best left alone. She might have had diarrhoea or wind. The boys could have found a novel way to keep her quiet. At least she could brush her hair before she went to the fish market.

I decided to try the breakfast room again and there they were, hair all nicely brushed. I asked if they'd left anything in the room. It turned out she wasn't a lady and it was her own brush. Apparently she was into hairbrushes. I guess there was no harm done.

Not everyone in Scotland was as hospitable as this lady though. Not long after the hairbrush tale, I'd left my brick of a mobile phone (remember, this was the mid-90s) on the boat and it was time to call the office for my morning call. I spotted a payphone not too far away and with a couple of ten pence pieces in my hand, I walked over to make my call.

It was one of those old analogue phones where you stuck your finger in the number you wanted and turned the dial. Luckily for me and my finger I hadn't started with '0' but '7' because, as I moved the dial round, I caught a glimpse of something shiny and stopped dialling. Some idiot had stuck an old-fashioned razor blade underneath the dial. It was positioned halfway across the '0' so that, if you'd completed the dialling process, you'd have cut the end of your dialling finger off. Just the thought made my bum go fizzy.

As I sat there in The Dickens shaking my head and laughing at the divers being divers at the bar, I thought to myself, 'That was you 30 years ago!' I made my decision at that moment to accept the job of operations manager for Rockwater and start a new exciting chapter of my life in March 1997.

35

Desk Jockey

IT didn't take me long to realise I wasn't really suited to working in an office. Exciting it was not. I hadn't been in charge for long when I got a phonecall from the IT department. Wait for it – some people had been looking at porn on their computers. A crime with summary dismissal attached to it.

From my experience offshore, we did have the odd peek if the weather was bad, but only to keep the reps company. Besides, looking at things like that used to put me off my food. There would have been no one left offshore if it had been the same out there – company reps watched it all day.

The HR department got involved and called me to say I'd have to be present at one of these meetings of summary dismissal. It turned out the guy was an up-and-coming engineer. He'd worked for me offshore, as had his girlfriend.

The lady in charge of HR was in my office ready to do the first interview with this lad. I asked what he'd been watching and asked how bad it was. It turns out Snow White and the Seven Dwarfs had been getting up to no good.

We were all sat around my desk, when this lad walked into my office. At this time I still thought it was a joke. I figured I'd have to give him a bit of a bollocking without grinning and send him on his way. Instead, he sat at the end of the desk and was read his last rites, told to go back to his office, clear his desk and leave the premises immediately.

I don't know who was more shocked – him or me.

It turned out that receiving porn on your computer was okay; looking at it was the crime. The guys in the IT department could tell if you'd opened it. What a bunch of sneaks.

Not only did we lose a promising engineer, but his girlfriend, who was also an engineer, decided to leave.

I asked my secretary to stop sending me stuff like that.

It was things like this, that pettiness of working in an office, that infuriated me. I was used to sorting things out on the spot, face-to-face. You either shaped up or you were shipped out. No sneaking around looking at other people's computers, waiting for Snow White and her mates to trip up. It was a new way of life and I figured it would take some readjustment.

At first, when I started as ops manager, I was a bit of a hero to some as I'd been there, done that. I don't think they realised that most of the hard work was done on the beach.

The business development guys would go out and find jobs. The commercial guys would go out and win the contracts. Then the engineers and draughtsmen would figure out how to do it and give it to a project manager who, with his accountant, would put the job together in a neat package complete with a profit ready to go offshore at the allotted time.

We'd have maybe six to a dozen jobs on the go at various stages at any one time, which took a lot of planning. We only had a certain number of vessels to do the work so it all revolved around the vessel schedule. We worked to the 'Six P' schedule: Proper Planning Prevents Piss Poor Performance.

Most of the time it worked. When it didn't, things got expensive. Most jobs we did were fixed price with liquidated damages if we didn't finish on time.

We weren't the only ones on a schedule – the oil companies we worked for would have shut-down periods ready for us to come in and do the work. They'd have to shut down production with a big loss of revenue. The pressure to get finished started before we even got on site. Luckily, the oil companies often took the weather risk.

One of our jobs had a £250,000-a-day liquidated damages set on it. The engineer on the job had got his calculations wrong when he measured the length of a spool. We tried to make it fit for a day then pulled it up when it wouldn't. We re-welded it, re-tested it, and re-fitted it. We ran three days over.

I was called to the engineer's cabin one morning as he refused to come out. When I went into his cabin he was in the foetal position at the end of his bunk, wailing. He'd cracked. I had to send him back to the beach and get another one. I later learnt that the first thing he did when he got back to his desk was open the Snow White attachment.

That's stress, believe me.

Those oil companies cut you no slack.

36

Safety

BETWEEN 1997 and 1999 I progressed from ops manager to general manager within the UK and then on to global offshore operations manager. So many titles in so little time. In my eyes, I was still a 'diving person'. Far less words and far simpler to describe.

As part of my career ladder climb, I was informed that I would be the champion for safety, who, wait for it, could be prosecuted for manslaughter if someone had an accident and got killed. Between this and Snow White, I thought, 'Put me back in a chamber for 28 days. Far easier and far better paid.'

At this point I no longer classified people as people. I immediately remember thinking there were 500 potential accidents walking about on the bottom of the North Sea in the mud and black water. As much as you could tell divers not to put their hands in any danger, or to keep their heads clear of swinging loads, there were still a heck of a lot of three-fingered divers about with sore heads. This safety thing was really not my bag.

We had a diver nip his finger on one occasion. I think he broke his nail. I was summoned to the oil company's headquarters, along with our health and safety guy and given a right working over. This went on for a couple of months. It cost all our profit in the job and then some. But it did get me focused. I even made a safety video that was shown worldwide.

I was fast becoming a star.

Years later I saw the same oil company got a £1m fine for blowing up an oil terminal. What goes around comes around.

After a while, I gradually became more office-orientated, albeit, I felt more at home on a barge or in a diver's outfit at the bottom of the ocean. Meeting after meeting, e-mail after e-mail and because we were part of a bigger organisation, I had a reporting line that took me down to London once a week. Once a month we had the knights of the round table meeting. This brought all the other heads of various parts of the company together.

Together we reported the progress we'd made and how close we were to the business plan that we'd set. The business plans from all the units contributed to the overall company business plan. It was all about how much profit we were going to make – profit made bonuses. I must tell those divers, I thought, to keep their fingers out of those holes as it was making me poor.

At first I was nervous doing these presentations, sat in this lovely office with all the other heads of companies. My secretary and the chief accountant in Aberdeen would put my presentation together for me and explain, as best they could, what I should and shouldn't say.

Don't put more on the table than you've promised, the accountant would tell me. They have this nasty thing called a 'stretch'. If you said, only once, you were able to beat your forecast, you'd soon find they'd be banking on it. I quickly realised it was best to leave some under the carpet for a rainy day.

The meeting would be held in various locations. Sometimes they'd come and see me in Aberdeen or we'd go to Stavanger in Norway; maybe even Houston in the States.

London was best.

I'd take the afternoon flight from Aberdeen to Gatwick where I'd be picked up in the limo and have a chat with the driver about which football pundit he'd delivered to Sky television that day and what monster-sized house they lived in.

Whoever's patch you were on would be responsible for the evening venue and would have to pick up the tab for the restaurant. One night we went to Princess Diana's favourite restaurant in Kensington. I had the sardine starter which cost £15, which consisted of only one sardine. No wonder she was thin.

We did go to some really nice restaurants when oil was $80 a barrel. We were making money and having fun. I was beginning to like my new job and the bonus that came with it. Then the price of oil started to slip.

It slipped so much at one time it was down at just below $10 a barrel, which in turn saw targets missed and bonuses flying out the window. The oil companies tightened their belts and put all their projects on hold until the price of oil went up again. It was time for us to do the same.

From above came the directive to stop all business-class flights, and all unnecessary travel costs were cut wherever possible. My immediate boss in London called me and said he'd be coming up to Aberdeen for a meeting to discuss what could be done to save money and asked if I'd pick him up from the airport and take him to his hotel where we'd have dinner. Lovely, I thought. It would save me cooking.

I picked him up and took him to the hotel. He checked in and said he was just taking his bags to the room and having a quick wash. Meantime, would I mind ordering a bottle of champagne before we had dinner? I could get the hang of this cost-cutting, I thought.

Stopping club-class travel was a bit of a nightmare, but it was going to save the company a vast amount of money so it had to be done. You were only allowed to travel business class if you had agreed it with the big boss in London. Special circumstances were required. Health was one and having to travel on the same day as the meeting you were attending was another. You were encouraged to travel a day early so you could rest up for your meeting.

Suffice to say this encouraged much scheming. We mostly all travelled business class and drank champagne when we travelled alone.

One day we all had to go to a meeting in Houston. This meant there'd be a lot of us on the same flight. No one had a good reason to travel business class.

The other problem was that we were already in Amsterdam having a meeting and the trip to Houston was an onward journey. KLM was the preferred carrier.

When it was time to board I used my platinum card to board early and went straight to my seat in business class. We'd only been up in the air a few minutes when Smudger came through from cattle class all irate and sat down in the empty seat next to me.

'How did you manage to get a business-class ticket?'

'I got a sick note,' I said. 'Bad back.'

I told the boss man I couldn't sit in one of those seats for seven hours with my back. He agreed. Sympathising, he said he had the same problem.

The stewardess asked Smudger to go back to his seat as we were just about to have our lunch with a nice glass of champers.

Later I came clean and told them the truth – I had so many air miles with KLM I had been upgraded before the flight.

I had to stay on in Houston after our meeting because I was head of the diving division. The company was changing the way it did its business. I'd been nominated to attend the seven-day introduction course about a computerised system called SAP. Funnily enough, at the time of writing this book, my son is helping to introduce the system into Jaguar Land Rover in Coventry.

Some $1.8m had already been spent on the computer system that was going to save the company millions. We were going to sack hundreds of people and save money. With the new system one man could order and pay for a bag of cement instead of the three it currently took. I sat there for two days and never understood a word they were talking about. On the third day I was on my way home to get my back looked at.

At the next meeting of the round table I was asked to give a speech on my thoughts about the introduction of SAP. Great! I didn't have a clue about this system and I think they knew that. Luckily or unluckily it looked like we were about to miss our budget so the focus was back on making more money – more money meant more bonuses.

After another million dollars and a failure to get SAP working it was scrapped.

37

Family

WITH all the changes in my career life going on, it was nice to get grounded for a few weeks as I got to focus on some family time.

Mum was over from South Africa where she lived in a lovely cottage on the third fairway of a secure retirement development.

She'd moved over to South Africa to be close to my sister who was married to a guy out there. Unfortunately, due to some bad investments by my brother-in-law, stress took over and my mum was popping anti-depressants as fast as she could eat them. My brother-in-law always looked after mum fantastically well, I just don't think he ever understood the stress and strain he caused everyone.

Mum, who was in her late 70s, suffered, and in the end had something of a nervous breakdown. She came over to the UK to recoup and visit her three sons as well as her other long-time friends. She'd come and stay with me which suited us all fine, seeing as I was the best cook.

During this particular visit she was in recovery mode. She was feeling frail and required peace, quiet and lots of love and affection. Thankfully my wife got on very well with my mother and looked after her that week, baking cakes together and taking them to her old friends.

I was back at the weekends, but those two days were pretty hectic for me. My love and affection had to go a long way. Even the grass had to have some but not before the pool had been cleaned.

Sunday was a great day. Nice dry grass cutting weather. The wife and mother were sitting in the garden reading the Sunday papers, while I was mowing the grass away, mulling over what I'd cook on the barbecue once I'd finished the lawn.

'Are you deaf,' my wife said, tapping me on the shoulder. 'Didn't you hear the phone ring?'

'No. The lawnmower must have drowned it out. Who is it anyway?'

'Jerry,' she said.

I got on the phone. 'Hi Jerry, how's it going?'

Jerry was one of the offshore superintendents. He was a good mate and knew he could call me anytime – even when I was at home cutting the grass.

'You're not going to like this,' he said. 'Your brother's had an accident. At the moment he's lying flat on his back in the middle of the deck, bleeding from both ears, his nose and with a gash on his head. It doesn't look good. The medics are having a look, but don't hold your breath. I'm going to order the Medevac helicopter from Bergen. Meantime, I'll keep you informed.'

My heart dropped through my body. To say I was wobbly was an understatement.

Jerry called me about every 30 minutes, updating me on progress and thank god, five or six calls later, my brother was still alive. They'd put him on a helicopter with a doctor heading for hospital in Bergen in Norway. Meanwhile, mum turned to me and said, 'Don't they leave you alone at weekends?'

I couldn't tell her that her oldest son was in grave danger of dying. That was the last thing she'd need to hear in her state. I decided she didn't need to know unless the worst happened.

Later she said, 'Robin always calls on a Sunday. I wonder why he hasn't called this week?'

I told her that his vessel was in a bad area for making calls. 'Reception is awful there. As soon as things improve I'm sure he'll call you.'

Meanwhile, I got our travel department to book me on the first flight over to Bergen. The first flight was Monday morning: Norwich to Amsterdam to Stavanger then, finally, to Bergen.

The operations manager in Norway had done a great job of keeping me up to speed with what was happening. He met me at the airport and we went to the hospital together. I was dreading what I might find.

Despite having lived my life as a strong-headed male, I'm not good at the sentimental stuff – I burst into tears at every occasion when it involves high-powered emotions. I even had to take tablets at my daughter's wedding. The irony, having lived my life as a diver with the mantra 'panic kills', was that these tablets were called 'Be Calm'. The doctors told me things were stable. Robin had broken his neck in several places and was in traction. You can imagine what I must have been like when I went into his room and saw him with his head being pulled one way and his body being pulled the other.

He kind of looked at me without moving his head and said, 'Give me a kiss, Dave.' Well, that did it. They had to give me a sedative to shut me up. Though at least he was alive and in a really good hospital surrounded by some very pretty nurses.

The doctors and nurses did a great job. They kept him there for a couple of weeks until he was deemed fit enough to be Medevaced back to the UK.

A few days later, I explained the mother problem to Robin. I'd not told her about the accident but she was getting concerned that she hadn't heard from him. Together we managed to get him to call her from his hospital bed without spilling the beans about what had happened, in addition to a further promise of a call the following week.

It was now getting to the end of her stay. Robin explained he wouldn't be back in time to see her before she went home. This seemed to do the trick and she seemed happy enough, though she did remark that he didn't sound like his normal self.

Over the following months he stayed in a couple of excellent hospitals in the UK, where they put some plates and screws into his neck and back. They also put a cage on his head, which gave him some traction, before finally letting him go home six months later.

I often wondered if I should have told mum the truth.

Eventually I did – a year later.

By then she was a lot stronger and took it well. She only cried a bit when he limped up to her with a cage screwed on to his head to keep him from moving it about.

During his recovery he had had lots of visits from his crew and people from the office, which I knew he'd appreciated and had helped keep his spirits up. I decided it would be nice to give him something to boost his spirits even further.

When he worked offshore he normally worked on the *Rockwater 1* vessel. So, with the help of the vessel manager Charlie Brown in Aberdeen, we purchased a three-wheeler bike and put the number plate 'Rocky 1' on it, loaded it into the company van, and took it south to his home in Eastbourne. Charlie and I flew down to make the presentation and took him and his wife out for dinner.

The dinner was fabulous and Robin had a great time as the wine flowed and tension evaporated. Although it seemed the wine had been evaporating at a steady rate that night.

The next morning I was in the dog house. His wife said he'd somehow fallen into the bath intoxicated. He'd had to spend the rest of the night in the bath as she couldn't lift him out. Oops.

He got a nice settlement from the insurance company which paid for his divorce, a gold Rolex, and a Porsche. With a lot of hard work and a little help from his friends he eventually returned to work on light duties selling the safety message, 'If it can happen to me, it can happen to you. You might not be so lucky.'

It was always hard to see anything bad happen to family, but I was especially tight with my siblings. My brothers and I all became saturation divers around the same time, and my older brother Robin was a bit of a local hero growing up, as he became British waterski champion in 1964. I just hoped this episode would be the last bad fortune to strike my family for a while, but I was way off the mark unfortunately.

Six months later, my youngest brother had a stroke from which he never recovered. Not a coherent word has since passed his lips or a single step taken to this very day.

He'd suffered with a bad case of the bends not long before the stroke but we could never get any medical evidence to say that it had contributed to the stroke in any way. No massive insurance payment for him.

Fortunately, he has a great wife who takes excellent care of him.

As one of three brothers who had all dived a great deal, I know I'm fortunate to have come away pretty much mentally and physically unscathed. That in itself is worth more than all the money and riches on the planet and if I did have unlimited wealth, if there was a way I could trade it for my younger brother's health, I'd do it in a heartbeat.

38

Treasure

MANY divers started out as mercenaries, especially at the time of wars – and there have been enough of those over the years. Treasure hunting soon became very popular, but over time, the type of gold that people have been more interested in, is liquid black.

With the drop in the price of oil, desperate measures were needed to maintain the bottom line and secure the much loved bonuses. Rockwater had just joined forces with another company called Subsea and were looking to increase the bottom line via a number of mediums. One of them was to reduce headcount.

When I took redundancy at Rockwater at the end of 1999, I wasn't allowed to work for anyone else for 12 months as I was placed on gardening leave. During that time they suggested, 'Why don't you go treasure hunting? We'll pay your expenses as normal.' Wasn't a bad deal really, so I accepted.

Over the years we'd dabbled in treasure hunting as far back as HMS *Edinburgh*, but on the whole we'd had little success. They did say that to make a small fortune in the treasure hunting game you had to start with a large one.

One day I got involved with a guy who'd made a large fortune. Here's how he did it. He'd been wandering around the USA and discovered Kentucky Fried Chicken (KFC). He subsequently bought the franchise, which turned out to be a big success, sold it, and made a big fortune.

He had a Rolls-Royce convertible with his own number plate, EFR. I asked what it stood for. Extremely Fucking Rich, he told me.

He spent a fair bit of time in the Philippines and ended up marrying a Filipino lady – a general's daughter. It would be his contact with the general that would eventually lead us to the very top of the Filipino hierarchy.

Over the years, all the shallow water wrecks had been plundered by President Marcos who needed the money to buy shoes for his wife. Sod the poverty.

When the Americans were chasing the Japanese out in the Second World War, the Japanese would plunder as much as they could and load it all on to their getaway vessels. These little vessels were then bombed and sank with all their treasure on board. There were an awful lot of them.

The KFC man came into my office one day with a proposal he'd obtained through his father-in-law's contacts. There were some very influential people who knew where one of these little boats had sunk with 27 tons of gold on board.

Around the same time, KFC man introduced me to another friend of his, who knew where there was an untold amount of treasure on a sunken galleon – again in the Philippines. I arranged to meet him at an airport that was convenient to us both.

You couldn't miss him – he was a treasure hunter for sure.

Sharks' teeth round his neck, little ponytail, and a sovereign ring on his finger. He told a good story about how they'd already found lots of stuff: cannons, plates and other debris. They'd even identified the galleon's superstructure which certainly resembled a Manila galleon.

Not a single Manila galleon had ever been found. This was exciting stuff.

These old galleons would have had the treasure loaded into the bottom of the hull and would have been covered with a layer of rocks to stop the crew from stealing it. The rocks would also act as ballast. If they encountered a storm and floundered on the rocks, the bottom of the boat carrying the treasure covered in rocks would get ripped off first long before the rest of the boat sank, leaving a trail of debris on the sea bed.

Finding the treasure which would still be covered in rocks was the tricky part. The weight of the rocks would push the treasure down into the sea bed and, over a period of time, be covered in sand or mud. Even finding the rocks would prove difficult: you'd have to be very lucky and maybe find a giveaway piece sticking out.

I did often wonder about an old nutty professor I crossed paths with in Aberdeen who could have held the key to treasure hunting of all forms. He invented a gadget which was going to be revolutionary, but never took off. It was like a wand which measured the atomic value of whatever you were looking at. For example, gold's atomic number is 79 and silver's is 49. If you were going over the rocks with this gadget, it would have identified anything on the particular setting of what you were looking for. The original intention was to allow oil companies to establish the location of oil instead of having to carry out seismic surveys. Used correctly, the individual or company could clear up. I don't know why the concept didn't get rolled out commercially as it was the strongest set of eyes on the planet.

I had dinner with the KFC guy in Singapore.

A living legend in his own mind but I did manage, through all the bullshit, to get the gist of what really happened.

It was time for me and my mate from Singapore to start taking this seriously. Rockwater had a big contract, building a giant platform in the Philippines which required several trips over for updates, progress reports, all that sort of stuff. The man who knew where the galleon was also knew the other people.

On our next trip, to the fabrication yard, we arranged to meet up in Manila.

If you've never been, let me tell you, there's a hell of a lot of people and poverty in Manila. Every time our car stopped at the traffic lights, a kid with a stump would put a bowl through the window with his other hand asking for money. I remember thinking you'd need a lot of money to feed this lot. Very sad. The country needed more than a few coins, it needed international aid. Once we got to the hotel and checked in, we gave our man in Manila a call and arranged to meet for dinner. After a lot more stumps and empty bowls, we arrived at our destination.

From the outside it didn't look much like a restaurant. Sure enough, once through the door, we realised they didn't sell food in this place. We were sat at the bar waiting for our man to turn up when, suddenly, through the door comes this Italian American guy called Greco, who was shouting at the top of his voice, 'There's a dog in the house! There's a dog in the house!'

This seemed to be the signal for all the girls to squeal with delight.

'Hello Mr Rue,' they all shouted in unison.

It would appear Mr 'Mad Dog' Rue was well liked in this place.

Greco, our man, made the introductions. Mr Rue turned out to be a really nice guy (ex-Delta Force) – he was doing bodyguard work for some of the high-up Philippine officials, hence the tie-in with the other people.

Before we went to the restaurant, they took us back to the apartment to show us what they'd already accumulated from their wrecks. I have to say, they had a very tidy collection which was going to be shipped over to Greco's warehouse in the States for safe-keeping.

Over dinner, Rue said he had some video footage of the sunken galleon that he'd like to show us. We arranged to meet up again the next day at his house for the show.

The video wasn't the best quality but you could make out the shape of the stern and the little castle-type features with the square portholes. My only recollection of what a galleon looked like was the one Captain Pugwash used to get about in. This one resembled it. Not much gets me excited, but this did.

We saw cannons laying on the sea bed, broken china and saw on closer inspection, what they said was the remains of three Philippine pipe divers who had got hung up on the wreck and drowned, probably within the previous few weeks or months.

This boat was on the sea bed, 240 feet below the surface. God knows how those pipe divers had even got down there. This is why they wanted us to bring the saturation boat over as it was out of diving range for the pipe divers. I figured they were all dead before they'd managed to recover a cannon.

It looked promising, so we agreed if the vessel schedule allowed for a quick stop-over, we would have a look and see what was down there, following the debris to the mother-lode. In essence, a piece of cake.

The next day, it was time to meet the bigwigs at the naval base to talk about the other wreck with the 27 tons of gold on board, which had been sunk in the Second World War.

When we arrived at the base we had to go through tight security before we even got to go into the meeting room. Once inside, you could see why.

The meeting was being chaired by the Admiral of the Philippine Navy and what looked like some other very important people. They told us that they knew the location of the wreck and that they even had an eyewitness who saw the boat get bombed and then sink. They went on to say that if we agreed to bring a boat in to recover the gold they would give us protection and immunity, which would remain in place all the way back to Singapore. With pirates all over the place in that part of the world, it was the kind of guarantee I felt we needed.

Once we'd recovered the loot, the top man would helicopter out, select what he wanted, and the rest would be ours. There was always a risk they could take the lot and we could return empty-handed.

That said, it sounded like a good deal.

Meeting over, we arranged for them to come over to Singapore to look at the vessel. They came over and had a look at the boat. Greco and Rue as well. There was lots of shaking of hands and backslapping. The gold was as good as ours. The bonus was in the bank.

We decided to do a little bit more research before we committed though.

I called a guy in Brisbane, Australia who'd done a lot of salvage work in this part of the world, just to see if he knew anything about this particular vessel.

It seems I'd interrupted his game of golf.

I always thought you had to turn your phone off when you were playing golf. That's what my wife tells me anyway.

In between puts he told me he had indeed heard of our boat with the gold and that he'd even had it surveyed ready to salvage.

Their kind of salvage was crude. They'd get over the top of the wreck and drop a big grab down, grab as much as they could, pull it up, and drop it on the deck then go through it later. Not exactly keyhole surgery.

He said the survey showed the vessel was still in one piece. They'd never got round to doing any work on it but that it was worth a shot. Our boat was due to finish its present contract in three weeks and return to Singapore. It was our slot.

John, the KFC mogul, and I flew to Manila together. He would come out to the vessel with me when it arrived. Meantime, we planned on meeting the father-in-law and check in with Greco and Rue to see if they had any news on the galleon.

John, through his father-in-law, had got them their salvage ticket. Part of the deal was that they'd get the museum involved to authenticate anything they salvaged. As far as I understood, his father-in-law was straight. He figured anything that was found would remain in the Philippines and be put on show. I remember thinking we'd better not tell him about the gold – the president might have him shot.

Greco had other ideas. He was boxing things up from his previous jobs and shipping them straight back to the States as fast as he could. At the time John didn't know this.

We met all the president's men for breakfast a couple of times. Everything looked good. Next day, we all travelled to a location where an old Japanese man would show us the exact location of the sunken boat.

On the bus, John had Googled the price of gold. He worked out, to the last dime, how much he was going to get as his share for setting up the introductions, and for the record it was a very healthy figure.

I could see our diving boat lying just offshore waiting for us to get on board. The old Japanese guy was in a hut on an intravenous drip. He'd given the location to the navy lads. The navy lads had enough ammunition to sink a battleship. I wouldn't like to be a pirate trying to nick any of the president's gold, I thought.

We piled into a big rubber assault boat and headed offshore to board our dive boat. Harry and the captain were waiting for us. I don't think the captain was quite expecting the assault force that appeared on his deck. He'd been warned, but I think he thought it'd be one person with a musket.

The navy lieutenant gave us the location and we prepared to put the ROV down to locate the wreck. The excitement was intense; the price of gold had gone up. John had to recalculate.

When we found the wreck, or what was left of it, they couldn't believe it. All that was left was a sheet of steel which used to be the bottom of the hull – someone had beaten us to it. Worse still, it had been crudely grabbed.

I hope he missed all his bloody putts, I thought.

We looked about, just in case we were on the wrong wreck, but in the end conceded defeat. The lieutenant had to make a tricky phonecall to the top guys from the Philippines. He then reboarded the assault boat and headed back to the beach. All in all, a disappointing journey, especially as my cut personally could have been a few million quid.

When I passed the hut with the old Japanese guy, I noticed the intravenous drip had been removed and he wasn't moving. He must have still been asleep. I figured the sleep on this occasion would last a long time. Those president's men were extremely pissed off.

While we were still on the dive boat I'd talked to John about the galleon job and the way Greco was going about things. I decided we'd have no part of it.

Just as well because someone opened one of the boxes he was shipping back to the States and arrested him – he's been in jail ever since. Mad Dog Rue sends him food parcels now and again. Only John knows what made the customs people look in a box.

To my knowledge, like the HMS *Edinburgh* back in the early 1980s, this galleon is still sitting on the sea bed laden with gold. In fact, there's a whole bundle of treasured wrecks just there for the picking…as long as you have a multi-millionaire to finance the operation.

One of the last treasure hunting adventures I was asked to do involved one of the most famous vessels in history – *Titanic*.

Keith (the guy who did all the research for HMS *Edinburgh*), had a son called Graham who was also into the treasure hunting scene. I got on well with Graham and cutting a long story short, we went out to the USA and won the contract to carry out the ROV work on the *Titanic*, in the hope that we could recover the bursar's safe, as there was supposedly some very valuable jewels inside.

To say I was excited was an understatement. I'd been promised a ride down in the *Calypso* submarine, so I could see the wreck first hand. I was even given a gift box, which contained a piece of coal from RMS *Titanic*, with its own little certificate!

Unfortunately my excitement was short lived, as the type of ROVs we had didn't cut the mustard. In brief, they were outdated and not in the best condition. And in an instant my visit to the *Titanic* was shattered. Nice while it lasted.

However, there's more to life than just money and globetrotting. The time to choose my priorities in life was fast approaching.

39

Granddad

I'M often asked what brought along my decision to retire. My answer is always, 'That trip to Bombay.' Unfortunately, this anecdote does not come loaded with action-packed tales of helicopters falling out of the sky, typhoons or 800lb grouper fish – far from it. I left from Norwich on a Tuesday, arriving in Bombay on a Wednesday. The meeting was something to do with a job I was doing in Bombay High (now Mumbai High), an oil field about 100 miles from Mumbai. I sat there for about four hours listening to people harping on about strategies and figures which made no sense whatsoever, and was back on a plane straight after, arriving back in Norwich on Wednesday evening. The whole trip was a waste of my time and energy. If the meeting had happened these days, it would most likely have happened over a video conference call or I would have simply received a document to sign, in order to proceed. Back then, it was essential for anybody holding a position to attend a meeting, even if it was resolved in five minutes. Pointless really.

I can't totally blame it on this one particular meeting though. There had been a few similar to this over the last couple of years and I guess this one put me over the edge.

As opposed to the early days when I used to love travelling, collecting my gin houses with KLM and experiencing new cultures, my outlook on life had changed. I realised that I had a beautiful house and home, with a great family, and that is where my focus now needed to be. If I travelled now, I needed to be doing so without any work strings attached, at my own pace and with my own agenda.

I turned to my wife on arriving home and said, 'That's it. I'm not doing this anymore.' I'd fallen out of love with something I used to have a great passion for. A 32-year innings wasn't bad though.

My gardening leave with Rockwater pretty much drew a line under my full-time employment within the commercial diving trade. When I left the offshore trade and started working with the onshore side of the business, the excitement of the job disappeared. The buzz starting to rapidly disappear.

I did a few jobs in Australia and the US afterwards in a consulting capacity, but certainly nothing which was worthy enough to make it into this book. Within a couple of years of finishing with Rockwater, at the ripe age of 55, I hung up the gloves.

My wife had a boutique, so while she was hard at work I transformed from deep sea diver to domestic maid, looking after the garden, the shopping and the cooking. Who would have ever thought eh? It wasn't a massive shock to the system though. My life for many years had involved me working for one month on, one month off. In essence, that month off at home was no different to being in retirement. The difference being, I used to have to get all my domestic duties sorted in a month, whereas now I have forever to do them.

I often get asked if I missed the whole guy bonding and camaraderie thing. The answer is no. Don't get me wrong, I made some good friends and have some great times to look back on, but I wasn't hooked on the whole alpha male side of life. In my opinion, and you may not believe it, that was just bullshit.

Nowadays, I get all the male bonding I need on a Thursday, playing golf in the seniors league at the local golf course which I am a member of. I play mainly with our old family doctor, a builder and a toyboy, but we do have some other interesting characters, including oil field hands, army officers and randomly ex-bugle and trumpet players. And then we have the bandits, you know who you are (comedians and retired bank managers!).

Golf is a sedate game at our age, yet very competitive. It's not uncommon to find a packet of discarded painkillers laying on the tee which has helped to ease a stiff joint, not that kind of joint. One day we were teeing off on the 12th when flying out of the car park with blue lights flashing and siren blaring came an ambulance. The driver was shouting out of the window, 'Which way to the 17th?' He was obviously not a member – we all know that's the second from last. One of the lads was down, but which one? It was too far to see. Some minutes later the ambulance made its way back and disappeared through the car park. No blue light or siren, we feared the worst. Turned out that he had had a heart attack. I remember thinking his ball must have landed on the green.

Luckily, with the aid of modern medicine and some fine doctors they put some stents in the arteries leading to his heart and he was swinging a club two weeks later. Excitement? It was a talking point for a couple of weeks! We were all glad that he made a full recovery. From my wreckage salvation days, I'm glad to say, I've now got a new name to replace 'Body Bag Beckett'. It's now 'Bend it like Beckett' – I slice.

Many unfortunately found it difficult to come to terms with life after diving. Many very wealthy divers still tried to live like playboys, only to go broke within a few years, become alcoholics or find it difficult to maintain a marriage. I had a distinctly different well-balanced life at home and that was perhaps my saviour. I have two incredible children called Guy and Victoria and three beautiful grandchildren called Oscar, Olivia and Madison.

My views on the diving industry now? It's still a risky business to anyone willing to dive deep under the surface and stay there for any given length of time. I believe technology has certainly assisted the industry and the measures to increase the levels of safety are on a totally different level to my days. The majority of commercial diving jobs now are actually diver-less. I'd even go as far as taking a guess that commercial diving may even be taken over by robotics in years to come, making divers obsolete. I may be part of a dying breed.

Fitness also plays a big part. When I first started in diving, I received a letter about three lines long from the doctor saying I had a good exercise tolerance, which basically meant I had jumped up and down for a few minutes on a stool, was given a cardiograph and a pat on the back to say I was good to go. Then they introduced a little blue book which was called the 'Diver's Fitness Register'. It had four columns on pages about six inches by four inches, which stated the date, name of employer, result of examination and a signature from an appointed doctor. The dialogue which accompanied the 'Result' column would have in-depth medical terms and descriptions such as 'Fit for diving work'. I kid you not. Divers these days have to undergo a battery of tests to prove they are fit enough to dive and the paperwork that accompanies that confirmation is in-depth. I'm happy things have tightened up on that front.

Something that hasn't changed and will always be an issue, is the mental health of divers. Thankfully I've never had any bad dreams or have been haunted by past events. It's as if the events are stored in a part of my brain which allows me to revisit the stories in graphic detail, but unless I make an effort to think about those events, or am asked a question, they stay fairly dormant in my head. Unfortunately for many, witnessing one bad event was enough to make them quit, or in some cases lead to their own downfall whether it be through suicide or being psychologically affected for the rest of their lives through post-traumatic stress. The post-diving support, especially for those doing body recovery, has gotten better over the years, but the support after needs to be stronger. There's too many old drunk divers sitting on bar stools around the world, telling their tales, who could have had a great life with the correct guidance and support at their time of trauma.

In terms of my career – I started at the bottom and ended at the top. Although the irony is, when I first started, I was aiming to start at the top and reach the bottom successfully. As a 20-year-old farmer boy from Norwich, I would have never thought 30 years later I would have been running one of the largest diving companies in the world. I'm happy with my journey and hope my grandchildren in years to come can tell my tales to their grandchildren and say, 'That was your great-grandfather, David Beckett. He was a deep sea diver.'